Sharjah

MINI VISITORS' GUIDE

www.explorerpublishing.com

الشارقة
Sharjah
هي وجهـتي
my destination

Dear Visitor,

On behalf of the Sharjah Commerce & Tourism Development Authority it gives me great pleasure to welcome you to the emirate of Sharjah, the cultural capital of the Arab world.

As one of the seven emirates which constitute the United Arab Emirates, Sharjah is a fascinating oasis. From majestic mountains and desert landscapes to beautiful beaches, it offers a distinctive blend of history and modernity, and a combination of east and west.

Nowhere quite embraces the old and the new like Sharjah; you can find over twenty museums, a centre for Arabian wildlife, superb facilities for sports, ancient souks, modern shopping centres, luxurious hotels and resorts, plus dining and entertainment venues, all well equipped to cater to the diverse needs of individual travellers, families and incentive groups.

Whatever you do, wherever you go in Sharjah you will encounter a warm welcome that reveals a living tradition of courtesy and hospitality. It is an adventure like no other. It is your destination.

We hope this guide will help you to discover the charm of Sharjah and leave you with cherished memories of a remarkable experience.

Enjoy your stay and *'Ahlan wa sahlan' – 'Welcome to Sharjah'.*

Sultan Bin Ahmad Al Qassimi
Chairman
Sharjah Commerce & Tourism Development Authority

Sharjah Mini **Visitors'** Guide 1st Edition
ISBN – 978-9948-450-12-2

Copyright © Explorer Group Ltd 2011
All rights reserved.

All maps © Explorer Group Ltd 2011

All images © Sharjah Commerce & Tourism Development Authority

Front cover photograph: Khalid Lagoon – Pete Maloney

Printed and bound by
Emirates Printing Press, Dubai, UAE

Explorer Publishing & Distribution
PO Box 34275, Dubai, United Arab Emirates
Phone (+971 4) 340 8805   Fax (+971 4) 340 8806
info@explorerpublishing.com
www.explorerpublishing.com

Welcome To Sharjah

Welcome to a unique destination, to a modern metropolis, a capital of culture and history, and a land of lagoons and beaches, desert and mountains.

It is hard not to be charmed the more you look into this extraordinary emirate. Sharjah's story takes you on a journey through some 5,000 years of history. From valuable archaeological sites to important ecosystems and pristine wilderness areas, there is an incredible natural history here. Cultural traditions play a central role in society, with respect for religion and heritage underpinning every aspect of modern life to the extent that it is no surprise that Sharjah has been named Capital of Islamic Culture for 2014.

The cultural attractions are indeed impressive. The array of museums, galleries and heritage areas (p.76) provide an unrivalled insight into Arabic history. It is also easy to soak up the culture by strolling amongst the traditional architecture, timeless dhows and atmospheric souks (p.150).

There is great shopping in the modern malls (p.156) and the souks are perfect places to bargain for souvenirs (p.149). Having always been a trading hub, there is a great array of goods to look out for (p.146). There are cafes and restaurants showcasing the best of Arabic, Asian and international food (p.172). With a great variety of places to stay (p.58) and sports and activities (p.120) on offer it is easy to explore. From diving to mountain biking, desert driving to dhow cruising, there is

Sharjah at dusk

something for everyone here; and Sharjah is also the perfect base from which to explore the rest of the Arabian Peninsula.

Over the next few pages, descriptions of the local culture and history should provide context to your trip. Following this is the vital information you'll need to get here and stay in style, plus advice on what to do when you first arrive. The things that you really shouldn't miss start on p.16. The Exploring chapter (p.64) divides the emirate up, highlighting each area's best bits, such as museums, galleries and heritage sites. In Sports & Spas (p.116) you'll find out what's on offer for active types, sports fans and those who simply prefer to be pampered. Shopping (p.140) is your detailed guide to souks, malls and stores, and Going Out (p.162) will help you through Sharjah's maze of restaurants, cafes and entertainments.

Culture & Heritage

Rapid change and growing multiculturalism hasn't stopped Sharjah from embracing its proud heritage to help define its future.

Sharjah's Story

Sharjah's rich history of human habitation stretches back over 6,000 years. Important archaeological sites have been discovered throughout the emirate that cover the Bronze and Iron ages and the pre-Islamic period. From an early existence based on subsistence farming and fishing, communities developed in structure and complexity as regional trade began to bring wealth. The arrival and development of Islam brought greater advances still, and the expansion of the Arab Empire brought influences from further afield. Varied cultures have played their part in Sharjah's history, from the Mongols and the Ottomans to the Portuguese and the British. The area that is now the UAE ultimately accepted British protection in 1892 following a series of maritime truces; so becoming known as the Trucial Coast (or Trucial States), a name retained until the departure of the British in 1971.

Growing Trade

Sharjah was for long the most important port in the region and a crucial trading hub. Sharjah city grew around the creek and facilitated trade between merchants throughout the Arabian Gulf, as well as being the trading post for Bedouins

from the desert interior who would come to the souks with bundles of charcoal and other goods. The east coast enclaves of Kalba, Khor Fakkan and Dibba played crucial and formative roles in the development of trade in the region. Seafaring expertise continued to reap rich rewards from the pearl beds, while busy fishing fleets operated on both coasts and in the hinterland farming continued around the oases. By 1932 Sharjah was the most important hub for a more modern type of transport when it opened the Gulf's first airport, a crucial staging post for commercial flights between Britain and India.

Independence

In 1968, Britain announced its withdrawal from the region and oversaw the proposed creation of a single state consisting of Bahrain, Qatar and the Trucial Coast. The ruling sheikhs realised that by uniting forces they would have a stronger regional presence. Negotiations collapsed when Bahrain and Qatar chose to become independent. However, the Trucial Coast remained committed to an alliance, and in 1971 the federation of the United Arab Emirates was born.

Formation Of The UAE

The new state comprised the emirates of Sharjah, Abu Dhabi, Ajman, Dubai, Fujairah, Umm Al Quwain and, in 1972, Ras Al Khaimah. Each emirate is named after its main town. Under the agreement, the individual emirates each retained a degree of autonomy. The leaders of the new federation elected the ruler of Abu Dhabi, HH Sheikh Zayed bin Sultan Al Nahyan, to be their president, a position he held until he

passed away on 2 November 2004. His eldest son, HH Sheikh Khalifa bin Zayed Al Nahyan, was then elected to take over the presidency. Despite the unification of the seven emirates, boundary disputes have caused a few problems. At the end of Sheikh Zayed's first term in 1976, he threatened to resign if the other rulers didn't settle the demarcation of their borders. The threat proved an effective way of ensuring cooperation, although the degree of independence of the various emirates has never been fully determined.

The Discovery Of Oil

The formation of the UAE came after the discovery of huge oil reserves in Abu Dhabi in 1958. The emirate has an incredible 10% of the world's known oil reserves. This discovery dramatically transformed the emirate. In 1974, Sharjah, which was already a relatively wealthy trading centre, began petroleum production with gas production following in 1982. The development of Sharjah's natural resources has always been continued alongside the development of associated industries. The considered approach has brought great reward through a diverse affiliated industrial sector, as well as through diversifying its position as a trading hub through the development of its ports on both the Gulf of Oman and the Arabian Gulf.

Culture

Sharjah is a modern cosmopolitan metropolis with deep-rooted traditions. Islamic customs are central to all aspects of culture today, as they have been throughout Sharjah's history.

Courtesy and hospitality are highly prized virtues and visitors are likely to experience the genuine warmth and friendliness of the local people.

The rapid economic development over the last 30 years, which was sparked by the reign of Sheikh Zayed bin Sultan Al Nahyan (the 'father of the UAE'), has changed life in the Emirates beyond recognition. However, the country's rulers are committed to safeguarding its heritage. They are keen to promote cultural and sporting events that are representative of the UAE's traditions, such as falconry, camel racing and traditional dhow sailing. Arabic culture, as seen through poetry, dancing, songs and traditional art, is encouraged, and weddings and celebrations are still colourful occasions of feasting and music.

Food & Drink

There are a great variety of cuisines available in Sharjah, with European and American options as well as more geographically local Asian and Arabian options. These flavours reflect the emirate's colourful history and the common Arabic dishes are shawarmas (lamb or chicken carved from a spit and served in a pita bread with salad and tahina), falafel (mashed chickpeas and sesame seeds, rolled into balls and deep fried), hummus (a creamy dip made from chickpeas and olive oil), and tabbouleh (finely chopped parsley, mint and crushed wheat).

There are also opportunities to sample Emirati food while in Sharjah. The legacy of the UAE's trading past means that local cuisine uses a blend of ingredients imported from Asia

and the Middle East. Dried limes are a common ingredient, reflecting a Persian influence; they impart a distinctively musty, tangy, sour flavour to soups and stews. Spices such as cinnamon, saffron and turmeric along with nuts (almonds or pistachios) and dried fruit add interesting flavours to Emirati dishes. Look out for Al Harees, a celebratory dish made from meat and wheat, slow-cooked in a clay pot or oven for hours, and Al Majboos, in which meat and rice are cooked in a stock made from local spices and dried limes. Fish is widely used in local cuisine, both freshly caught and preserved. Al Madrooba is a dish which uses local salted fish, prepared in a thick, buttery sauce.

Among the most famed Middle Eastern delicacies are dates and coffee. Dates are one of the few crops that thrive naturally throughout the Arab world and date palms have been cultivated in the area for around 5,000 years. The serving of traditional coffee (kahwa) is an important social ritual in the Middle East. Local coffee is mild with a distinctive taste of cardamom and saffron, and it is served black without sugar. It is considered polite to drink about three cups of the coffee when offered.

Muslims are not allowed to eat pork and pork is not available in the emirate of Sharjah. All meat products for Muslim consumption have to be halal, which refers to the method of slaughter.

Alcohol is also considered haram (taboo) in Islam. It is not allowed in Sharjah and there is a zero tolerance policy so that visitors do not make the mistake of bringing anything in from elsewhere.

Religion

Islam is the official religion of the UAE and is widely practised, however there are people of various nationalities and religions working and living in the region side by side.

In Islam, the family unit is very important and elders are respected for their experience and wisdom. It's common for many generations to live together in the same house.

Muslims are required to pray (facing Mecca) five times a day. Most people pray at a mosque, although it's not unusual to see people kneeling by the side of the road if they are not near a place of worship. The call to prayer, transmitted through loudspeakers on the minarets of each mosque, ensures that everyone knows it's time to pray.

Friday is the Islamic holy day, and the first day of the weekend in Sharjah, when most businesses close to allow people to go to the mosque to pray and to spend time with their families. Many shops and tourist attractions have different hours of operation, opening around 14:00 after Friday prayers.

During the holy month of Ramadan, Muslims abstain from all food, drinks, cigarettes and unclean thoughts (or activities) between dawn and dusk for 30 days. In the evening, the fast is broken with the Iftar feast. At the top hotels and restaurants special Ramadan tents are put up and every evening an array of food and drink is served for those breaking their fast. These tents are usually filled to the brim with people of all nationalities and religions enjoying the evenings with traditional Arabic mezze, sweets and drinks. Ramadan is a special time in Sharjah and a fantastic occasion for visitors to

learn more about local culture and religion. Educational and entertaining events are held throughout the emirate.

The timing of Ramadan is not fixed in terms of the western calendar, but depends on the lunar Islamic calendar. During Ramadan shops and parks usually open and close later. Ramadan ends with a three-day celebration and holiday called Eid Al Fitr, the feast of the breaking of the fast.

National Dress

In general, the local population wear traditional dress in public. For men this is the dishdash(a) or kandura: a white full length shirt dress, which is worn with a white or red checked headdress, known as a gutra. This is secured with a black cord (agal). Sheikhs and important businessmen may also wear a thin black or brown robe (known as a bisht or mishlah), over their dishdasha at important events. You'll sometimes see men wearing a brimless embroidered hat (kummah), which is more common in neighbouring Oman.

In public, women wear the black abaya – a long, loose robe that covers their normal clothes – plus a headscarf called a sheyla. The abaya is often of sheer, flowing fabric and may be open at the front. Some women also wear a thin black veil hiding their face and/or gloves, and some older women wear a leather mask, known as a burkha, which covers the nose, brow and cheekbones. Underneath the abaya, women traditionally wear a long tunic over loose fitting trousers (sirwall), which are normally heavily embroidered and fitted at the wrists and ankles.

Tradition and heritage in Sharjah

Modern Sharjah

The emirate today is reaping rich rewards for its considered development and is a leading Middle Eastern hub for commerce and tourism.

Through careful investment, Sharjah has managed to make the most of its natural resources, geographic location and cultural charms. The infrastructure throughout the emirate is impressive and facilitates ongoing growth.

As well as increasing numbers of tourists, Sharjah is also seeing an influx of investors, entrepreneurs, expatriate workers and students. The industrial sector is thriving, the free zones at the airport and ports are seeing increasing investment, businesses are setting up throughout the emirate and the University City continues to shine as a bright beacon of academic excellence.

Tourism

The continued development of high-end hotels and visitor attractions, in conjunction with an articulate international information campaign, has made Sharjah a popular holiday destination. It has become the region's cultural getaway of choice and with a busy and impressive roster of festivals throughout the year it appeals to visitors as an event destination.

Hotel occupancy increased through 2009 and 2010 despite the impacts of the global financial slowdown. With

new events and developments planned it is likely that the emirate's popularity will continue to grow.

New Developments

There are ongoing projects that are designed to further improve Sharjah's offerings for the future. In August 2010 construction began on the first phase of the 'Heart of Sharjah' project which is designed to markedly transform the areas of and surrounding the Heritage Area and Arts Area. Historic buildings are to be renovated and rebuilt. The area's souks are to be upgraded with air conditioning and modern facilities while retaining their heritage charm. There will even be a boutique hotel established in one of the famous old houses. The emirate's art scene continues to develop apace and the area is set to become a perfect home to future Sharjah Biennials. The culturally sensitive development will make the most out of the existing heritage architecture while augmenting it with considered construction projects, all designed to create an area of great appeal to visitors, residents and investors alike.

Meanwhile construction projects continue with impressive municipal buildings being erected throughout the emirate and further development of business and tourist projects. In the Al Hamriyah enclave the Nujoom Islands development is well underway. It is a unique project where the islands are natural, not man-made, and the water channels are carved out. Already attracting significant investment, the development promises a bold new world of waterside living for Sharjah.

Sharjah Checklist

01 Tackle The Dunes

The great desert that distinguishes the Arabian Peninsula is a fantastic and fascinating destination. A great playground for all kinds of adventure, Sharjah's sand dunes are perfect for off-roading, camel trekking, sand skiing, fossil hunting or even just picnicking. See p.126

02 Sample The Souks

Sharjah's shopping secrets are in the enthralling and absorbing souks. As well as being a great insight into tradition, and offering fantastic photo opportunities, they are great for souvenirs. Head to Central Souk or Souk Al Arsah for the best choice of carpets, textiles jewellery and other treasures. See p.150

03 Explore Old Sharjah

The creek-side Heritage Area is an unmissable
attraction. Just to walk among the coral stone
buildings and labyrinthine passages is to step back in
time some 200 years, before the discovery of oil, when
Sharjah was the most important port in the region and
wealthy on trade, seafaring and pearls. See p.76

04 Life's A Beach

With coast on both the Arabian Gulf and the Gulf of
Oman, Sharjah has beaches galore. In the city, there
are beaches perfect for picnicking, and hotel beaches
for swimming and watersports. Over on the east coast
there are the long empty sands at Kalba and the fun-
filled crescent bay of Khor Fakkan. See p.104

05 Get Your Cultural Fix

With its collection of world-class museums, galleries and attractions Sharjah's cultural scene is flourishing and makes for a top cultural getaway. From classical to contemporary, don't miss the amazing Museum of Islamic Civilization, the Art Museum and the Maraya Art Centre. See p.71

06 Explore the East Coast

There is a world of adventure on the east coast, from the craggy peaks of the Hajar Mountains to sleepy beaches, pristine mangroves and amazing underwater habitats. Try mountain biking and hiking in the hills, kayaking at Khor Kalba, and diving and snorkelling in the incredible aquarium world. See p.98

07 Entertain the Kids

A fascinating and friendly place for all the family,
there are attractions and activities to suit all ages.
The museums are all purposefully arranged to appeal
to children, while the parks are full of play areas and
indoors there are a host of amusement centres. Don't
miss the outdoor funfair of Al Jazeera Park. See p.71

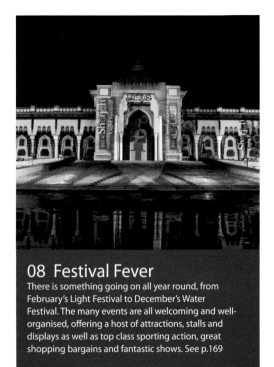

08 Festival Fever

There is something going on all year round, from February's Light Festival to December's Water Festival. The many events are all welcoming and well-organised, offering a host of attractions, stalls and displays as well as top class sporting action, great shopping bargains and fantastic shows. See p.169

09 Wow at the Wildlife

Get up close to the critically endangered Arabian Leopard at the inspiring Arabian Wildlife Centre, face up to incredible sealife at the Aquarium, let the kids pet the animals at the Children's Farm and Posh Paws Animal Sanctuary or head to Khor Kalba and see if you can spot the rare kingfishers. See p.102

10 Enjoy Al Qasba

Along the banks of the canal, between palm trees and wooden bridges, Al Qasba is the place to be. Sweeping walkways link the alluring cafes, restaurants, shops and galleries. Take a ride on the Eye of the Emirates, peddle a four-wheel cycle, cruise in an abra, dance with the fountains – or just chill with an ice cream. See p.170

11 Hit The Water

There are watersports galore on both coasts. Take a jetski off Al Mamzar lagoon, or from Khor Fakkan on the east coast. Go sailing from any of the beach hotels. Try your hand at big-game fishing in the Gulf of Oman. Or just take a peaceful dhow ride through the city's lagoons. See p.70

12 Declare Paintball War

Let loose your military side at the Sharjah Golf and
Shooting Club. With an impressive floodlit setup that
features dense undergrowth, bunkers, hills, trenches,
parked jeeps and even an old aeroplane it is no
wonder that this paintball park is regarded as one of
the very best in the Middle East. See p.127

Visiting Sharjah

A warm welcome awaits visitors to Sharjah and the UAE, but there are a few rules and regulations that warrant extra attention.

Getting There

Sharjah International Airport (SHJ) was the original aviation gateway to the UAE. The first airport opened in 1932 to serve as a stopover point for Imperial Airways passenger planes en route to India and Australia. Air travel has come a long way in the last eighty years and the modern airport which greets travellers to Sharjah now is a far cry from the desert outpost of yesteryear. Thanks to its central position between both the Far East and Europe, and Dubai and the Northern Emirates, Sharjah International Airport is an increasingly popular choice for UAE arrivals and departures and for transit passengers; as well as being the region's favoured cargo hub. In 2009, almost five million passengers passed through the airport on their way to 280 destinations worldwide. The airport offers a good range of facilities including banking, a medical clinic, children's play area, business centre,

> **Airport Info**
>
> The main phone number for Sharjah International Airport is 06 558 1111. For assistance with lost and found items call 06 508 4297, open 24 hours. For further information see www.sharjahairport.ae

Sharjah International Airport

Sharjah Airport Hotel (06 558 1110) and Duty Free access for arrivals, departures, transit and transfers. Hala Services (www.halaservices.ae, 06 558 1100) can be booked to provide round the clock assistance to passengers with special needs, unaccompanied minors, the elderly and those going through Immigration and Customs formalities; arrivals and departures lounges and porter services are also available.

Sharjah's award winning Air Arabia broke new ground in the region when, in 2003, it was launched as the Middle East and North Africa's first low-cost carrier. This popular airline now flies to 40 destinations from its Sharjah hub and Sharjah Airport's 20 minute check-in and check-out times no doubt add to the appeal, making it a favourite for a short getaway!

Airport Transfer

If your holiday has been booked through a hotel or travel agency in Sharjah, you may find that pick-up from the airport is included. If not, there are a number of options available to whisk you away from the airport. Airport buses run on a number of routes to downtown Sharjah and to Dubai, linking with the Dubai bus network at Al Qusais bus station and with Dubai Metro at Rashidiya Station – one bus an hour runs from

Airlines

Air Arabia	06 558 0000	www.airarabia.com
Air France	04 602 5400	www.airfrance.ae
American Airlines	04 316 6116	www.aa.com
British Airways	800 0441 3322	www.britishairways.com
Emirates	06 569 0759	www.emirates.com
Etihad Airways	06 577 0333	www.etihadairways.com
Fly Dubai	04 301 0800	www.flydubai.com
Gulf Air	06 568 3766	www.gulfairco.com
KLM Royal Dutch Airlines	800 556	www.klm.com
Lufthansa	04 373 9100	www.lufthansa.com
Oman Air	06 574 8212	www.oman-air.com
Qatar Airways	06 569 1818	www.qatarairways.com
Royal Brunei Airlines	04 334 4884	www.bruneiair2.com
Royal Jet Group	02 505 1500	www.royaljetgroup.com
Singapore Airlines	06 568 4411	www.singaporeair.com
South African Airways	04 397 0766	www.flysaa.com
United Airlines	800 0441 5492	www.united.com
Virgin Atlantic	04 406 0600	www.virgin-atlantic.com

06:00 to 22:00 with an increased service at weekends and on public holidays (fares are Dhs.15 from Sharjah to Dubai and Dhs.10 from Dubai to Sharjah). The express bus service from the airport to Al Ittihad Terminal runs every 45 minutes while the local route to Al Sharq Terminal runs every 15 minutes (both cost Dhs.5 and run from 05:30 to 23:30), see www.mowasalat.ae.

Taxis are plentiful in Sharjah and for those leaving the airport, the tariff starts at Dhs.20, with an additional Dhs.20 added to the metre fare if crossing into other emirates. A journey to downtown Sharjah will cost around Dhs.50.

Visas & Customs

Requirements vary depending on your country of origin. Regulations are subject to change and should be checked before departure. GCC nationals (Bahrain, Kuwait, Qatar, Oman and Saudi Arabia) do not need a visa to enter Sharjah. Citizens from many other countries get an automatic visa upon arrival at the airport. The entry visa is valid for 60 days and can be renewed for a further 30 days, at the immigration department. Visitors from countries that do not get an automatic visa need to apply before travelling; this can be done through some airlines or by the hotel that you will be staying at. A transit visa (up to 96 hours) is available to those travelling on Air Arabia with a confirmed onward booking,

Duty Free
The allowances for passengers arriving in Sharjah are 2,000 cigarettes, 400 cigars or 2 kg of tobacco.

on any international carrier, to a destination other than that of their original departure.

Certain medications, including codeine, Temazepam and Prozac, are banned even though they are widely available in other countries. High profile court cases have highlighted the UAE's zero tolerance to drugs. Even a miniscule amount in your possession could result in a lengthy jail term. Baggage will also be scanned to ensure you are not carrying any magazines or DVDs deemed offensive.

Dos & Don'ts

The UAE is one of the region's most tolerant states, carefully balancing traditional Muslim values with the innate desire to welcome visitors. Visitors to Sharjah should be aware though that as a traditional emirate, lewd behaviour is not only disrespectful but can lead to arrest and detention. There is a UAE wide zero tolerance to drinking and driving (p.34), something to bear in mind if spending an evening in a neighbouring emirate where alcohol is available; Sharjah being 'dry'. Visitors should also be aware that, in keeping with Sharjah's 'Decency Code', revealing clothing is not acceptable and both men and women should be covered from shoulder to knee. Public displays of affection are not permitted.

It is polite to ask permission before photographing people, particularly women. Smoking is common, however, new laws have been introduced banning smoking in some public spaces including malls and some restaurants so it's best to check the policy before lighting up.

Al Noor Mosque

Local Knowledge

Climate

Sharjah has a subtropical and arid climate. Sunny blue skies and high temperatures can be expected most of the year. Rainfall is infrequent, averaging only 25 days per year, mainly in winter (December to March). Summer temperatures can hit a sizzling 48°C (118°F) between June and September. From November to March average temperatures range between 30°C and 14°C, perfect for beach days and alfresco evenings. For up-to-date weather forecasts, see www.shj-airport.gov.ae.

Crime & Safety

Crimes against tourists are a rarity in Sharjah, and visitors should enjoy feeling safe and unthreatened. A healthy degree of caution should still be exercised, however, and most hotels offer safes to keep your valuables locked away in. To avoid a great deal of hassle make sure you keep one photocopy of your personal documents with friends or family back home and one copy in your hotel safe. Sharjah Police will advise you in the event of a loss or theft. If you lose your passport, your next stop should be your embassy or consulate; many are to be found in neighbouring Dubai. If you lose something in a taxi, call the relevant taxi company (p.53). Extra caution should be taken on the roads, whether navigating the streets on foot or in a vehicle. Use designated pedestrian crossings and make sure that all cars are going to stop before you cross.

There is zero tolerance, UAE wide, towards drink driving, even after one drink, and if you're caught you can expect a fine and a spell in prison. With plenty of low-cost taxis around, there's no excuse or need.

Electricity & Water

The electricity supply is 220/240 volts and 50 cycles. Most hotel rooms and homes use the three-pin plug that is used in the UK. Adaptors are widely available and only cost a few dirhams. Tap water is desalinated sea water and is perfectly safe to drink but most people choose mineral water for the taste. Bottled water is cheap and widely available.

Money

Credit and debit cards are accepted around Sharjah. Foreign currencies and travellers' cheques can be exchanged in licensed exchange offices, banks and hotels (a passport is required when exchanging travellers' cheques). Cash is the way to go in souks, markets and smaller shops. The monetary unit is the dirham (Dhs.), which is divided into 100 fils. The currency is also referred to as AED (Arab Emirate dirham). Notes come in denominations of Dhs.5 (brown), Dhs.10 (green), Dhs.20 (light blue), Dhs.50 (purple), Dhs.100 (pink), Dhs.200 (yellowy-brown), Dhs.500 (blue) and Dhs.1,000 (browny-purple).

The dirham has been pegged to the US dollar since 1980, at a mid rate of $1 to Dhs.3.6725.

Sharjah Police

Sharjah Police are well respected and active within the community and very approachable. For assistance, call 06 563 1111 or visit Sharjah Police website, www.shjpolice.gov.ae/en/index.html. In case of emergency call 999 for police or ambulance and 997 for fire.

People with Disabilities

The requirements of visitors with special needs are beginning to be considered more carefully in Sharjah but, in general, facilities are limited. Sharjah Airport has provision for travellers with special needs, including the Hala service which can be booked in advance. Most of the newer malls and hotels should offer accessible rooms.

Public Toilets

You will find plenty of clean, modern, western-style toilets in the modern malls and tourist attractions but there is a lack of public bathrooms in souks and older attractions. Facilities can be pretty basic so carrying tissues will come in handy.

Telephone & Internet

Temporary SIM cards for mobile phones work on a pay-as-you-go basis. You can buy a package from Du online (www.du.ae) or at its outlets in major malls. For Dhs.55 you will get a welcome bonus of Dhs.20, usage bonus of Dhs.100, and lifetime validity. Etisalat's 'Ahlan' package costs Dhs.60, includes Dhs.25 credit, and lasts for 90 days with an extra 30 day grace period when you can only receive calls; it is available from malls and Etisalat offices. You can easily buy top-up cards for both packages from petrol stations, supermarkets and newsagents. Mobile phone numbers in the UAE begin with a prefix 050, 056 (both Etisalat), or 055 (Du).

Wi-Fi is available in some hotels, and most include use of a business centre (sometimes for a fee) where there are computers and internet access.

Time

The UAE is four hours ahead of UTC (Universal Coordinated Time, formerly known as GMT). There is no altering of clocks for daylight saving in the summer, so when Europe and North America lose an hour, the time in the UAE stays the same.

Offices and schools are closed on Fridays (the holy day) and Saturdays and most malls and attractions won't open until after prayers on Fridays.

Tipping

Tipping practices are similar across hotels, restaurants and cafes in Sharjah with most people adding 10% to their bill. It is standard in taxis and at petrol stations, but not compulsory, to round up to the nearest Dhs.5.

Useful Numbers

Police	999
Ambulance	998/999
Fire	997
Traffic Emergency	06 563 4444
Airport Taxi	06 508 1143
Al Madina Taxi	06 533 4444
Delta Taxi	06 559 8598
Union Taxi	06 532 5333
Sharjah Airport	06 558 1111
Flight Information	06 558 1555
Directory Enquiries	181
UAE Country Code	00 971

Language

Arabic is the official language of the UAE, although English, Hindi, Malayalam and Urdu are widely spoken. Most signs and menus are in Arabic and English. The further out of town you go, the more you'll find only Arabic written and spoken. Arabic isn't the easiest language but if you can throw in a couple of words here and there you're likely to receive a smile.

Basic Arabic

General

Yes	na'am
No	la
Please	min fadlak (m)/min fadliki (f)
Thank you	shukran
Praise be to God	al-hamdu l-illah
God willing	in shaa'a l-laah

Greetings

Greeting (peace be upon you)	as-salaamu alaykom
Greeting (in reply)	wa alaykom is salaam
Good morning	sabah il-khayr
Good morning (in reply)	sabah in-nuwr
Good evening	masa il-khayr
Good evening (in reply)	masa in-nuwr
Hello	marhaba
Hello (in reply)	marhabtayn
How are you?	kayf haalak (m)/ kayf haalik (f)

Fine, thank you	zayn, shukran (m)/zayna, shukran (f)
Welcome	ahlan wa sahlan
Goodbye	ma is-salaama

Introduction

My name is...	ismiy…
What is your name?	shuw ismak (m) / shuw ismik (f)
Where are you from?	min wayn inta (m) / min wayn (f)

Questions

How many / much?	kam?
Where?	wayn?
When?	mataa?
Which?	ayy?
How?	kayf?
What?	shuw?
Why?	laysh?
And	wa

Numbers

Zero	sifr
One	waahad
Two	ithnayn
Three	thalatha
Four	arba'a
Five	khamsa
Six	sitta
Seven	saba'a
Eight	thamaanya
Nine	tiss'a
Ten	ashara

Newspapers & Magazines

There are several English language newspapers published in the UAE and available in Sharjah. *The National, Khaleej Times* and *Gulf News* (all Dhs.3) are broadsheets that cover local and international current affairs. *7 Days* is a free daily tabloid which covers local and international news, cinema listings, gossip and a widely read letters page. The UK broadsheet, *The Times*, publishes an international edition which is available daily from most supermarkets for Dhs.7.

Live Work Explore is Explorer Publishing's monthly lifestyle magazine for expats. It lists upcoming events, gives the low-down on living and working in the UAE and lets you in on the secret spots around the Emirates. It is available in most bookshops and supermarkets for Dhs.10.

Many of the major glossy magazines are available in Sharjah, but if they're imported from the US, Australia or Europe, you can expect to pay at least twice the normal cover price. All international titles are examined and, where necessary, censored to ensure that they don't offend the country's moral codes.

Alternatively, you can pick up the Middle East versions of popular titles including *Harper's Bazaar, Grazia, OK!* and *Hello!* where you'll find all the regular gossip and news, with extras from around the region.

Television

Most hotel rooms will have satellite or cable, broadcasting a mix of local and international channels. You'll find MTV, all the major news stations and some sports, documentaries and

BBC programming, in addition to the standard hotel room information loop.

For programming with a local flavour, check out City7, Dubai TV, Dubai One and MBC, all of which broadcast Arabic soap operas, talk shows and American sitcoms and dramas, in addition to locally produced shows. There are also channels showing camel racing and other local sports and events.

Radio

Catering to the UAE's multicultural audience, there are stations broadcasting in Arabic, English, French, Hindi, Malayalam and Urdu. Daily schedules can be found in newspapers. There are a good range of English-speaking stations to choose from. Tune into Dubai 92 (92.0 FM), The Coast (103.2 FM), Virgin Radio (104.4 FM), Channel 4 (104.8 FM), Emirates Radio 1 (104.1 FM) and Emirates Radio 2 (99.3 FM) for music or Dubai Eye (103.8 FM) for talk radio and sport. All stations broadcast regular news and traffic updates.

More Info?

If you want to know more about what's going on in the UAE, check out www.explorerpublishing.com for event listings and the Explorer community forum. If you want to head out of the city during your stay, pick up a copy of *Weekend Breaks Oman & the UAE* for the lowdown on the region's best hotels. The *UAE Off-Road Explorer* is as essential as sunscreen if you fancy heading out to explore, while the *UAE Road Map* will help you find your way back.

Public Holidays & Annual Events

Public Holidays

The Islamic calendar starts from the year 622AD, the year of Prophet Muhammad's migration (Hijra) from Mecca to Al Madinah. Hence the Islamic year is called the Hijri year and dates are followed by AH (AH stands for Anno Hegirae, meaning 'after the year of the Hijra'). As some holidays are based on the sighting of the moon and do not have fixed dates on the Hijri calendar, Islamic holidays are more often than not confirmed less than 24 hours in advance. The main Muslim festivals are Eid Al Fitr (the festival of the breaking of the fast, which marks the end of Ramadan) and Eid Al Adha (the festival of the sacrifice, which marks the end of the pilgrimage to Mecca). Mawlid Al Nabee is the holiday celebrating the Prophet Muhammad's birthday, and Lailat Al Mi'raj celebrates the Prophet's ascension into heaven. During Ramadan, food and beverages cannot be consumed in public during the day and smoking and chewing gum is prohibited. Women should dress more conservatively and you'll find the month a quieter more reflective time.

Public Holidays

UAE National Day 2011	Dec 2 (Fixed)
Islamic New Year's Day	Dec 7 (Moon)
New Year's Day 2011	Jan 1 (Fixed)
Mawlid Al Nabee	Feb 15 (Moon)
Lailat Al Isra & Mi'raj	Jun 28 (Moon)
Eid Al Fitr (3 days)	Aug 30 Moon)
Eid Al Adha (4 days)	Nov 6 (Moon)

UAE National Day

Annual Events

Throughout the year Sharjah hosts an impressive array of events, from well-respected international cultural festivals to family-friendly shopping and entertainment shows and world-class sporting events.

Sharjah Spring Promotions   January to February

Various Locations

Sharjah Spring Promotions is a great time to visit the city with amazing discounts, offers, raffles and prizes in all the major malls. There are cultural exhibitions, children's shows, games and activities.

Exhibitions

The Sharjah Expo Centre is the venue of choice for many exhibitions throughout the year. The government actively encourages MICE (meetings, incentives, conferences and exhibitions) tourism and there are more events every year. Many of these exhibitions welcome visitors with shows, stalls and special offers. See www.expo-centre.ae for information.

Sharjah Light Festival   February

Various Locations

This exceptional landmark event is a light extravaganza. An illumination of the city's landscape and buildings in a unique combination of light and music.

National Career Exhibition   February

Expo Centre

Exhibition for the UAE banking and financial sector.

Sharjah Light Festival

Perfect Wedding Show

March

Expo Centre

All brides-to-be, excited couples and proud parents should
head to this popular show that brings together all the best
and latest in wedding related products and services.

Sharjah Theatre Days

March

Heritage Area

This longstanding celebration of Sharjah's theatrical tradition
promotes traditional storytelling practices, retells classical
stories and showcases new work with performances aimed
at all ages.

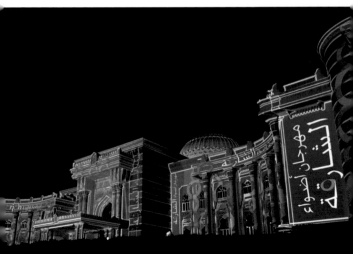

Sharjah Biennial   March-April
Various Locations
Every other year cutting-edge contemporary art visits
Sharjah in a two-month long show that leads the region's
artistic conversation.

Sharjah Heritage Days   April
Heritage Area
A two week celebration of Sharjah's cultural heritage with
events throughout the Heritage Area, displays of traditional
art, dance and handicrafts.

MidEast Watch & Jewellery Show   April
Expo Centre
Biannual exhibition showcasing the latest designs and trends
in watches, jewellery, gold, precious stones and diamonds
with exhibitors from all over the world.

The Art of Arabic Calligraphy   May
Sharjah Calligraphy Museum
Biennial exhibition that includes work from over a hundred
international artists, featuring a variety of styles and
techniques.

Family Fun   May
Al Qasba
One of the most popular times of the year for families with
events to entertain children of all ages, including puppet
shows, clowns, a funfair and boat rides.

Sharjah Summer Promotions   June-July
Various Locations
Summer in the city is easy with the amazing discounts, offers and prizes at this shopping festival.

Ramadan Fair   Ramadan
Expo Centre
Entertainment event for all the family with promotions, fun rides, raffle draws, entertainers, a heritage village and several restaurants. Open every evening.

Ramadaniat Al Qasba   Ramadan
Al Qasba
Religion, culture and history are celebrated in a series of events and activities to educate and inspire. There are art demonstrations and lectures in both English and Arabic.

Camel Racing   October-April
Near Al Dhaid
This popular local sport is an unmissable sight. Morning races take place throughout the winter between 07:00 and 08:30. Admission is free.

Sharjah World Book Fair   October-November
Expo Centre
One of the oldest and largest book fairs in the Arab World showcases thousands of titles in Arabic, English and other languages, displayed by private collectors, publishers, governments and universities.

Al Qasba Food Festival November

Al Qasba

There is always something going on down by the canal at
Al Qasba, but when the Food Festival is on there is an even
greater buzz with a host of cooking demonstrations, offers
and plenty of delicious things to try.

Sharjah Water Festival December

Al Majaz Park

Sharjah's premier all-family, all-action carnival attraction
features an enormous array of attractions. It is a kids
playground with rides, shows, exhibitions and workshops, as
well as a night souk and food court.

UAE National Day December

Various Locations

Every 2 December, the whole country turns green, black, red
and white all over. In fact, the flag becomes as ubiquitous as
fireworks, parades and traffic jams to celebrate the birth of
the UAE.

F1 Powerboat World Championships December

Khalid Lagoon

This major international sporting event is the climax of
both the Sharjah Water Festival and the F1 Powerboat
Season. Described as akin to driving a Formula 1 car across a
ploughed field, it makes for one of the most spectacular and
exciting sporting events in the world.

Sharjah has a busy calendar of exciting events

Getting Around

With a new fleet of buses, a plentiful supply of taxis and the chance to get out and explore on foot, getting around Sharjah is easier than you think.

Sharjah's traffic is a hot topic. You may have heard tales of long commutes, dodgy taxi journeys and summer dashes to avoid the sun but recent advances in Sharjah's public transport network are helping to smooth the way. Joining the plentiful and cheap metered taxis is a modern fleet of buses that criss-cross the city and, for a truly local flavour, a flotilla of water taxis (abras); Sharjah is a great place to investigate by foot too, especially in the cooler winter months. If you prefer to be in the driving seat then hiring a car is a great way to get out and investigate beyond the city.

Journey Planner

The best way to work out your public transport options is to use either the Sharjah Public Transport Corporation (www.stc.gov. ae) or Mowasalat (www. mowasalat.ae) websites. For further information, call Sharjah Transport on 7000 6 7000.

Bus

Sharjah's recently launched fleet of public buses run 14 routes daily, across the city, from 05:30 to 23:30. Known as Mowasalat, they sport a hard to miss orange livery. The buses are modern, clean and air-conditioned but can be crowded at peak

times. There is reserved seating on every bus for women and children. The main bus station is the Al Ittihad Terminal in the heart of the city. Cash and Sayer Smart Cards (see below) are both accepted, with standard fares costing up to Dhs.5. For further information call KGS PTS, the bus operator (600 522 282), Sharjah Transport (7000 6 7000) or check the website (www.mowasalat.ae) for route plans and fare information.

Airport buses, inter city buses and inter emirate buses are all available. Departing from the Sharjah City Terminal at Al Jubail Bus Station, services run throughout the day from 05:30 to 23:30. For more information, see www.stc.gov.ae.

Cycling

A lot of care is needed when cycling in the UAE as some drivers pay little attention to other cars, let alone cyclists. The winter is the most pleasant time of year for cycling. Keen road cyclists will enjoy the coast-to-coast route, while mountain bikers will find plenty of tracks in the Hajar mountains.

Driving & Car Hire

The best way to explore the city and entire emirate is by car, but driving in the UAE requires considerable care and attention. Driving is on the right and it is important to always be ready for the unexpected and to use mirrors and indicators. It's a good idea to keep the details and phone number of your destination handy in case you need directions en route.

Weekends are quieter but during the week rush-hour traffic jams are the norm, with the major city centre roads

busy all day and the Sharjah to Dubai highway particularly bad at peak commuting times. It is also worth avoiding the industrial areas if you can.

International car rental companies, plus a few local firms, can be found in Sharjah. Prices range from around Dhs.120 per day for a small car to Dhs.1,000 per day for a limousine. Comprehensive insurance is essential; make sure it includes personal accident coverage. To rent a car, you are required to produce a copy of your passport, a valid international driving licence and a credit card. There's plenty of free parking at malls, most visitor attractions and some of the tower blocks have underground parking but street parking can be a bit of a challenge.

In the unfortunate event of an accident, call the traffic police (Anjad, 563 4444) but do not move the car until they have arrived and assessed the situation. Most petrol stations are open 24 hours but many only accept cash, even in the shops.

Car Rental Agencies

Avis	06 559 5925	www.avisuaecarhire.com
Budget Rent-a-Car	06 572 7600	www.budget-uae.com
Diamond Lease	04 343 4330	www.diamondlease.com
EuroStar Rent-a-Car	04 266 1117	www.eurostarrental.com
Hertz	06 532 0113	www.hertz-uae.com
National Car Rental	04 283 2020	www.national-me.com
Thrifty Car Rental	06 574 0499	www.thriftyuae.com

Sayer Smart Card

The Sayer Smart Card is a rechargeable card being introduced to take the cash out of bus fares. It's currently available from Al Ittihad Terminal and Al Jubail Terminal (more outlets to follow). There is a one time Dhs.5 charge for the card then journeys paid for with the card cost up to Dhs.4.50 (rather than Dhs.5). The current balance is displayed on the ticket you receive. If the card is lost or stolen it can be disabled by calling 600 522 282 with the card's number.

Taxi

There are nearly 5,000 metered taxis, operated by five franchisees, plying their trade on the streets of Sharjah emirate. Fares start at Dhs.3 within Sharjah city and Dhs.2 in the Central and Eastern regions, making them cheaper than in most international cities. A minimum fare of Dhs.10 is being introduced and the pickup charge from the airport is Dhs.20; there is a Dhs.20 charge for inter emirate trips.

Taxis can be flagged down by the side of the road or you can order one through Sharjah Transport by calling 600 545 455. It always helps to carry a map or the phone number of your destination in case you hail a driver who's new to the city.

Adventure Travel

Beyond the city, the wilder reaches of the emirate are suited to adventurous exploration, from off-roading across the desert to hiking in the Hajar mountains, kayaking in the mangroves or diving amongst the rich sealife. See Sports & Spas (p.116).

Walking

The car is king in most of the UAE and summer temperatures of more than 45°C are not conducive to a leisurely stroll. The winter months, however, make walking a pleasant way to see Sharjah.

Khalid Lagoon (p.70) is popular even in the warmer months for an evening stroll. With wide promenades and plenty to look at, Al Qasba (p.170) is a favourite with families; and what better way to end your stroll than with a coffee overlooking the canal while the children play in the dancing fountains. The Heritage Area (p.76) and Arts Area (p.76) are also best explored on foot. Woven into the streets that line the creek, it is easy to spend a day wandering between the excellent museums and galleries, stopping off for a spot of shopping and a juice at Al Arsah Souk (p.152).

Street Strife

To make navigation more confusing, places may not always be referred to by their official name. For example, Sheikh Humaid Bin Saqr Al Qassimi Square is often better known as Flying Saucer Roundabout. District spellings vary within the city and roundabouts are called 'squares'.

Water Taxi

Within Sharjah city, the best option for getting a fresh perspective is to take a water taxi, or abra, at Al Qasba (p.170) or on Khalid Lagoon. Enjoy the city lights shimmering on the water and take in the canal, the lagoons and coastline. Abra rides cost Dhs.10 for adults and Dhs.5 for children at Al Qasba.

Sharjah is a fascinating place to explore

Essentials

Further Out

With cheap, modern, air-conditioned inter emirate public buses, affordable taxis and modern highways, there are the wonders of the East Coast and six other emirates to explore.

Visitors heading to Dubai have the choice of Metro, taxi, bus or water bus. The Red Line of the Dubai Metro opened in September 2009 and runs from Rashidiya to the airport, and down Sheikh Zayed Road, terminating at Jebel Ali; the Green Line, running from Al Qusais to Jaddaf, is expected to open in August 2011. Trains run from 06:00 to 23:00 from Saturday to Thursday, and from 14:00 to 24:00 on Fridays; at intervals of 3 to 4 minutes at peak times. The Metro's journey takes it past some of Dubai's top attractions. A Nol Card (see below) is the only way to pay for Metro, bus or water bus journeys in Dubai.

For those visiting Palm Jumeirah, a monorail runs from Gateway Towers station on the mainland to Atlantis hotel. Trains run daily from 08:00 to 22:00 and tickets cost Dhs.15 for a single fare or Dhs.25 for a return.

As well as the inter emirate buses, Abu Dhabi and Dubai are also serviced by cheap, modern local bus systems. For information on Dubai's public transport routes, see the Road & Transport Authority's (RTA) online journey planner at http://wojhati.rta.ae or call the RTA on 800 9090; you'll need a Nol card (see below) for bus fares. For information on buses in Abu Dhabi, call 800 55 555; the buses use the Ojra Bus Pass which can be bought from bus stands and Red Crescent kiosks on Abu Dhabi island.

The Emirates road network is modern but the driving can take some getting used to. Dubai has introduced a road toll

system, Salik. There are currently four gates, on Al Garhoud Bridge and Al Maktoum Bridge, and on Sheikh Zayed Road at Al Safa and Al Barsha. The toll for passing beneath one of the gates is Dhs.4 in a private car and Dhs.5 in a hire car. Passengers in a Sharjah taxi will have the Dhs.4 added to the fare, Dubai taxis are exempt from the toll.

Traditional water taxis, abras, still ply Dubai's creek. Crossing the creek by abra is a must-do experience for visitors to Dubai, with fares costing only Dhs.1 each way. If the abras seem a little basic, a fleet of high-tech, air-conditioned water buses have recently been added; fares cost Dhs.4 per trip. These can be hired for 45 minute creek tours which cost around Dhs.25 per person.

If you're heading out of the cities and planning a trip to the Musandam Peninsula or into Oman (p.113), it is vital to carry your passport as you will be crossing international borders. Some nationalities are able to apply for a visit visa at the border but visit the Royal Oman Police website (www.rop.gov. om) for up to date information.

Nol Card

Nol cards are convenient, rechargeable travel cards which can be used to pay for public transport and street parking in Dubai. The red Nol card is aimed at tourists and occasional users. It can be charged for up to 10 journeys, but is only valid on one type of transport, bus, Metro or water bus. The silver card is a better option if you plan to use different types of transport and the gold card provides access to the Gold Class Metro carriages.

Places To Stay

Along the beaches, around the lagoons and even over on the Gulf of Oman, Sharjah has great hotel options to suit all visitors and all budgets.

From five-star luxury to simple hideaways there are perfect spots for an exotic beach holiday, efficient business bases and ideal options for long-term stays. There are resorts all along the beachfront. Around Khalid Lagoon are some of the finest high-rise hotels as well resort options on the eastern shore. There are more hotels downtown, at the airport and farther out of the city. Over on the east coast at Khor Fakkan is the iconic Oceanic Hotel, while the Breeze Motel is a charming place overlooking the creek in Kalba. There are also hostels and fully furnished hotel apartments as less expensive options for those on a tight budget or looking to stay for a longer time period. Most places will offer concierge services, food outlets and a gym and swimming pool.

Rates vary through the season, so it is always worth checking for the best available rate and looking out for discounts and promotions. Online booking can often offer the best price, but it is always advisable to also check directly with the hotel. Most hotels can help to arrange airport pick-ups, but are likely to require a credit card and passport copy to confirm a reservation. A room tax is often added to the published rate, internet access can also be an extra charge and be aware that breakfast is not normally included.

Coral Beach Resort

www.coral-international.com
06 522 9999   **Map** 1 K2
A perfect white beach, plenty
of activities and sports facilities,
a spa and hammam, and in
Casa Samak (p.174) just about
the best fish restaurant and
seaside sunset spot in town.

Corniche Al Buhaira

www.millenniumhotels.com
06 519 2222   **Map** 1 D2
This luxury hotel stands tall
and proud in prime position
on Khalid Lagoon. There is a
rooftop swimming pool and a
fitness centre complete with
squash court.

Golden Tulip

www.goldentulipsharjah.com
06 519 7777   **Map** 1 D3
This hotel has a great location
just a short stroll from the
delights of Al Qasba, Al Majaz
Park and the Corniche with
some fantastic views of the
lagoon and fountain.

Holiday Inn

www.holidayinn.com

06 559 9900 **Map** 1 E3

The rooftop swimming pool is the crowning glory of this efficient hotel which also has a gym, sauna and full business facilities. Set just a couple of blocks from the south east corner of Khalid Lagoon.

Holiday International

www.holidayinternational.com

06 573 6666 **Map** 1 E2

A sprawling grassy complex on the banks of Khalid Lagoon and within walking distance of the Central Souk, this is essentially a country club in the heart of the city and it is good value too.

Lou' Lou'a

www.louloubeach.com

06 528 5000 **Map** 1 D1

This friendly beach club hotel has beach sports and watersports available, from sailing to parasailing, as well as fishing trips and beach volleyball games.

Places To Stay

Radisson Blu Resort
www.radissonblu.com
06 565 7777　　**Map** 1 G1
An icon of Sharjah, this is a classy, fun and luxurious five-star beach resort. There is a stunning private beach, full spa and the city's best al fresco dining spot, Calypso (p.173).

Rotana
www.rotana.com
06 504 4510　　**Map** 1 F1
This towering hotel is to the north of the creek and has full facilities including a good looking pool and fitness centre, efficient business setup and impressive buffet restaurant.

Royal Beach Resort & Spa
www.alkhalidiahtourism.com
06 536 5550　　**Map** 1 D1
On a great location overlooking the beach this resort has an old fashioned sense of luxury. There are opulent rooms, a traditional Russian restaurant, two swimming pools and a spa.

Sharjah Carlton Hotel
www.mhgroupsharjah.com
06 528 3711   **Map** 1 C1
Set fair right on the beach, this
well-organised old favourite has the
full array of activities with a great
pool and everything from tennis to
fishing available for guests.

Sharjah Grand
www.sharjahgrand.com
06 528 5557   **Map** 1 D1
Right by the sea, with 220 rooms
and an extraordinary array of
entertainments this is a complete
beach retreat. From parasailing
to karaoke, sumptuous buffets to
banana boat rides, it is all here.

Sharjah Premiere
www.sharjahpremiere.com
06 528 2777   **Map** 1 D1
With its beachfront location,
outdoor swimming pool and
rooftop fitness centre, this hotel is
perfect for active holidaymakers. It
also has business and conference
facilities for those on a working visit.

Other Places To Stay

Budget

For those on a budget there are many options including atmospheric choices such as the Italian themed Verona Resort (www.veronaresort-sharjah.com, 06 522 8820) and the Russian themed Al Corniche Hotel (www.villaalisa.com, 06 522 5235). Hostels are simpler and cheaper still; try Sharjah Hostel (06 522 5070), Sharjah Heritage Hostel (06 569 7707) and Khor Fakkan Hostel (09 237 0886). Visit www.uaeyha.com for more information or email uaeyha@emirates.net.ae.

Hotel Apartments

For longer-term stays furnished hotel apartments can be rented on a daily, weekly or monthly basis. These are available throughout the emirate at all price points; try Landmark Suites Hotel (www.lmhotelgroup.com, 06 742 9999), Royal Crown Suites (www.royalcrownhotelshj.com, 06 556 1333) and Ruby Living Courts (www.layia.net, 06 593 2222).

East Coast

Over on the east coast the Oceanic Hotel in Khor Fakkan (p.106) is an iconic property overlooking the crescent shaped bay. With a private beach, rooftop restaurant and an array of activities available (specialising in diving and fishing trips) it has long been a popular option.

Further south, overlooking Kalba creek, the Breeze Motel (p.98) is a charming little place with simple rooms, a small pool and gardens, and a fantastic grill cafe.

Exploring

Explore Sharjah

From captivating souks and museums to majestic mountains and incredible coastline, Sharjah is a place of cultural, historical and natural adventure.

With an extraordinary landscape and fascinating attractions there is the opportunity for all kinds of adventure in Sharjah. Rightly famed as one of the capitals of Islamic culture, the museums are world-renowned, the galleries are a hotbed of the renaissance in regional art, and the restored historical architecture is an attraction in its own right. The varied landscapes include impressive city parks, celebrated wildlife attractions, and desert, mountains and coast on both the Arabian Gulf and the Gulf of Oman.

City life is focused on the area around the lagoons, along the creek and on the coast. While it is easy to navigate and walk your way, the distances mean that the easily available buses, taxis and even small dhows are useful to take the strain from your legs. Taxis are a very easy way of exploring the city and surrounding area, but to make the most of the east coast a car is useful.

Explore the entire length of the Corniche (p.70) to stretch out on the beaches and soak up the atmosphere of markets, passing through parks and alongside lagoons. There are impressive museums and attractions here and at the famed Heritage and Arts Areas (p.76), where the concentration of history, education and entertainment is intoxicating.

Sharjah's Central Souk by night

Continuing the theme of exploring Sharjah's past and future, there are museums and attractions throughout the rest of The City (p.84) that concentrate on the areas of science and technology.

Out Of The City (p.90) the themes become wilder and there are incredible natural history attractions and a remarkable ancient landscape to explore. The emirate is unique in having land on both east and west coasts, as well as large swathes of precious hinterland. The East Coast (p.98) itself is a unique and special place. It is wild with wildlife, the atmosphere inviting, the activities exciting. It is an unmissable attraction for any visitor to the region.

At A Glance

Art Galleries

Beaches & Parks

Heritage Sites

Museums

The Corniche

Stretching all around the lagoons and along the creek, Sharjah life is focused on the Corniche with beaches, parks, souks, museums and canalside Al Qasba.

It is impossible to not be charmed by Sharjah as you explore the Corniche. The noble seafaring history is always in evidence, from the very geography to the many dhows and the impressive Maritime Museum. Culture is also on proud display, from antique craftsmanship in the souks to cutting edge art, in the Maraya Art Centre. This is indeed a cultured lifestyle, nowhere more so than along the canal at Al Qasba.

Beaches
The white sand, palm tree fringed beaches are great attractions for walkers, picnickers and photographers. For swimming and watersports head to any of the beach hotels, all of which will allow visitors to use their facilities for a fee. The long Al Khan beach is broken up by the hotel sections but there is still a long public stretch. On the other side of the creek, towards Ajman, the public beach is interrupted by the fishing harbour which conveniently means that a delicious seafood picnic can be found at any of the nearby cafeterias.

Lagoons
Sharjah's three lagoons, fringed with palm trees and skyscrapers, bobbing with dhows and jetskis, are at the heart

of Sharjah life. Khalid Lagoon is the showpiece, complete with the stunning Al Noor Mosque on its eastern shore. The towering fountain is the third highest in the world, reaching 100 metres, and erupts from 16:00 till 22:00 in a spectacular display that is colourfully illuminated after dark. The paths around the lagoons are popular with walkers and joggers. Dhow cruises can be taken from several points, while jetskis can be hired from the western side of Al Mamzar Lagoon.

Maraya Art Centre
Al Qasba
06 556 6555
www.qaq.ae

One of the region's leading venues for contemporary art, the Maraya complex is a social and artistic hub. There are regular lectures and workshops as well as exhibitions. On the first level The Shelter is a centre for local artists and creatives to work, network and enjoy the cafe and library. In collaboration with the Barjeel Art Foundation, the permanent The House of Arab Art exhibition on the second level showcases the finest Middle Eastern art. On the top level the Contemporary Art Gallery features regularly changing exhibitions. Open from 10:00 (16:00 Fridays) to 22:00. **Map** 7 G10

Parks
The most famous of all Sharjah parks is Al Jazeera. On the central island in Khalid Lagoon, it has been entertaining since 1979. Generations have grown up amongst its palm trees, pathways and attractions. The 250,000 square metre parkland includes a theme park's worth of bright lights and exciting rides. There are go-karts, boats and a train,

as well as a swimming pool, a log flume and a small zoo. Centrally located at the base of Khalid Lagoon, Al Majaz Park is popular for its geometric lawns and stunning central mosque. The parks are all well equipped with lawns, play areas and shaded seating. They open from 16:00 to 22:00, and have ladies-only evenings.

Al Qasba
06 556 0777
Nr Al Khan Lagoon
www.qaq.ae

The heart of modern Sharjah and its cultural hub, Al Qasba is busy with an ever-changing events calendar that includes poetry readings, film viewings and musical events. Cafe culture is strong here and – with families out for a stroll, students for a get-together, diners, shoppers and gallery-goers – it is always full of life. The 60 metre high observation wheel, the Eye of the Emirates, oversees it all and offers amazing views from its air-conditioned pods. **Map** 7

Sharjah Aquarium
06 528 5288
Al Khan
www.sharjahaquarium.ae

With an impressive setting right on the ocean, this world-class aquarium draws big crowds. Through tunnels, over bridges and past great fishtank walls, the displays are all designed to appeal to young and old alike. With over 250 types of marine creatures on show, the aquarium presents the full story of Sharjah's underwater world. A cafe, restaurant and gift shop add to the attraction. Opens at 08:00 (16:00 Fridays) and closes at 20:00 (21:00 Fridays and Saturdays). Closed Sundays. Dhs.10 for children, Dhs.20 for adults. **Map** 1 C1

Sharjah Maritime Museum

Al Khan

06 522 2002
www.sharjahmuseums.ae

The location is perfect: on the site of the old fishing village at the entrance to Al Khan lagoon, with two restored forts and the aquarium as neighbours. Inside and out the museum preserves and interprets the artefacts and stories of Sharjah's rich maritime heritage. Walk around restored dhows and get up close to models of the full range of vessels to better understand the seafaring history. Fishing, trading and pearling all had differing demands and much original equipment is on display along with genuine Arabian pearls. Opens at 08:00 (16:00 Fridays) and closes at 20:00 (21:00 Fridays and Saturdays). Dhs.4 for children, Dhs.8 for adults, Dhs.20 for families. **Map** 1 C1

Souks

More than just shopping, the enthralling and absorbing souks are attractions in their own right, great for photos and souvenirs. Head to the fish souk and fruit and vegetable souk early in the morning or late in the day to appreciate the region's colourful produce and to whet your appetite. Nearby, the plant and pot souk is a gentler place with plants and clay ornaments for sale. Along the creek by the Arts Area, Souk Al Bahar generates an atmosphere of chaotic frenzy, dealing in all manner of goods for the dhows which line the creek and ply their trade throughout the Gulf. The Central Souk and Souk Al Arsah are shopping and cultural destinations to not be missed; see page 150. The souks are generally open from 07:00 to 13:00 and from 16:00 to 23:00.

Exploring

If you only do one thing in...
The Corniche

Head down to Al Qasba for a relaxed cafe lunch, explore the shops and galleries, take a ride on the Eye of the Emirates and stay for dinner, people-watching and to soak up the atmosphere.

Best for...

Culture: For a full artistic fix, head to the Maraya Art Centre and lose yourself in the exhibitions, library and cafe.

Eating: Try the Lebanese specialities at Shababeek, an exceptional Lebanese restaurant in Al Qasba.

Families: Sharjah Aquarium is a great attraction for the whole family with exhibits and access designed for all ages.

Outdoor: Al Jazeera Park is famed throughout the region for its theme park attractions and long, peaceful lagoon-side paths.

Clockwise from top left: Khalid Lagoon's fountain, Etisalat-Eye of the Emirates, Sharjah Aquarium

Heritage & Arts Areas

Preserved in time, this is Sharjah before the discovery of oil, when it was the most important port in the region and wealthy on trade, seafaring and pearls.

Take a tour through the Heritage Area and be inspired by the architecture and simplicity of a lifestyle that thrived long ago. Sharjah has established itself as a centre for heritage in the United Arab Emirates and continues to keep its history alive by incorporating tradition into contemporary development – and nowhere is this more evident than in the Heritage Area.

To wander along the Sharjah Wall and in amongst the restored buildings is to walk back in time some 200 years. All the buildings have been lovingly restored and are now open as a series of museums, a theatrical centre and an important mosque. The museums typically open from 08:00 (16:00 Fridays) till 20:00, with free entry for children.

Just along the creek, the Arts Area is gathered around the impressive Sharjah Art Museum (p.78) which has played such a fatherly role in encouraging the current renaissance in Arab art and displays the very best modern and traditional work. The artistic effect can be seen in the immediate surroundings where galleries, craft shops and artistic suppliers thrive. Towards the mouth of the creek the great gilt dome of the Sharjah Museum of Islamic Civilization (p.80) should draw every visitor to its quite brilliantly educational and entertaining story.

Traditional architecture in the Heritage Area

Bait Khalid Bin Ibrahim

Heritage Area

06 568 0606
www.sharjahmuseums.ae

The house of this family, one of the leading pearl merchants in the Gulf, shows the distinct Bahraini styles of architecture and lifestyle. Antique exhibits are displayed in the courtyard and throughout the various rooms. **Map** 6 A8

Bait Al Naboodah

Heritage Area

06 568 1738
www.sharjahmuseums.ae

The home of the important and influential Al Shamsi pearl trading family, this former residence demonstrates traditional Sharjah ways of life from an era before electricity and air conditioning. **Map** 6 B9

Emirates Fine Art Society
Arts Area

06 568 4488
www.arts.ae

The society's attractive courtyard is open to visitors and there is a regular series of workshops, seminars and lectures to help promote art education and art appreciation among the public.
Map 6 D9

Al Eslah School Museum
Heritage Area

06 568 4114
www.sharjahmuseums.ae

The Al Eslah School Museum is the emirate's faithfully restored first classroom. Kept as it would have been a lifetime ago in 1935, pens still stand in inkpots on the wooden desks, verses from the Quran adorn the walls, and upstairs is a dormitory where foreign students would have slept.
Map 6 C9

Majlis Al Midfaa
Heritage Area

06 568 3030
www.sharjahmuseums.ae

Look out for the round windtower; it is the only one of its kind in the UAE and so effective as a precursor to air-conditioning - drawing any breeze down through the house - that the majlis was for long the city's cultural hub and meeting place. The museum explains the role of a majlis in society with artefacts and information displays. **Map** 6 B9

Sharjah Art Museum
Arts Area

06 568 8222
www.sharjahmuseums.ae

A destination gallery and museum, this is the family home of regional art and has hosted countless international

exhibitions. For over 15 years it has championed Arabic art, from cutting-edge contemporary to old-world classical, launched local talents and hosted blockbusting touring shows. A permanent gallery upstairs displays an unrivalled collection of pieces marking the first regional interactions with European visitors. Contemporary exhibitions in the downstairs galleries celebrate the hottest in regional talent and offer a fresher perspective on the region. There is also a great art library, gift shop and cafe. Open from 08:00 (16:00 Fridays) till 20:00. Entry is free. **Map** 6 D9

Sharjah Calligraphy Museum
Heritage Area

06 569 4561
www.sharjahmuseums.ae

This, the region's sole museum dedicated entirely to calligraphy, introduces the calligraphic tradition, the joining of poetry and art, of craftsmanship and philosophy, of Quranic teachings and today's tastes. Calligraphies of all styles, all eras and from all corners of the Muslim world are gathered. As well as being an ancient art form, modern calligraphers now often exhibit alongside graffiti artists and calligraphy is collected as an abstract art as well as a representational script. The museum is also a setting for both children's classes and adult education. **Map** 6 B9

Sharjah Heritage Museum
Heritage Area

06 568 0006
www.sharjahmuseums.ae

An amazing collection of exhibits tells fully how this area survived and thrived before the discovery of oil. Ancient coins that seem bashed flat by time evoke trades past. Costumed

mannequins, large-scale photographs and a selection of jewellery, pottery and other artefacts bring to life a past when fishing, farming, pearling and then maritime trade drove the economy. **Map** 6 A8

Sharjah Hisn (fort)
Heritage Area

06 568 5500
www.sharjahmuseums.ae

Once home to the ruling Al Qassimi family, the fort stands just 200 metres from the creek; proud, straight-walled and well-set – as it has for many generations – but now assimilated into the city, dwarfed by multi-storey buildings and with traffic speeding around it. Inside are priceless royal artefacts and the story of 200 years of history. **Map** 6 C9

Sharjah Museum of Islamic Civilization
Nr Sharjah Creek

06 565 5455
www.islamicmuseum.ae

The history here is the full story of Islamic civilization, exciting and interactive in this world-class, one-of-a-kind museum. Like Sharjah itself, the museum's approach mixes the old and the new. Exhibits range from the latest ladies' fashions to precious ancient manuscripts. The collection of over 5,000 exhibits spanning 1,400 years includes working models, robotic toys, scientific innovations, stunning jewellery and fabulous costumes. The museum is beautiful, educational and fun. There are prayer rooms, a cafeteria, gift shop and plenty of parking, including designated spaces for visitors with disabilities. Wheelchair access and bathroom facilities are available for visitors with disabilities, and there are also

View of the famous Majlis Al Midfaa windtower

baby changing facilities. Entry is Dhs.5 for adults, Dhs.10 for families. Open from 08:00 (16:00 Fridays) to 20:00. **Map** 1 F1

Souk Al Arsah
Heritage Area

The oldest marketplace in the UAE, this souk is still a special place. For years the gathering place of traders from throughout the Arabian Gulf and across the Indian Ocean, it was here that the Bedouin came with their camels and cargoes of charcoal, trekking to the coast from deep in the desert. It was here that charcoal was traded for the silks, rices and spices that merchants had brought from faraway lands. Today it is a great souvenir shopping destination and there is a great cafe as well; see page 173. **Map** 6 B9

If you only do one thing in...
Heritage & Arts Areas

Get lost amongst the labyrinthine passages of the Heritage Area and let the remarkable architecture bring the past to life; make sure you end up at the cafe in Souk Al Arsah.

Best for...

Culture: The full story of Islamic history, culture, art and religion is brilliantly told in the Museum of Islamic Civilization.

Eating: The cafe at the Sharjah Art Museum is a fantastically cultured spot with a full art library attached and a great range of teas, cakes and snacks.

Families: The Heritage Museum is great fun for all ages, with mannequins, models and curios.

Shopping: One of the finest places to buy authentic souvenirs, Souk Al Arsah is a must visit.

The City

Downtown Sharjah offers a fascinating insight into an impressive record in the fields of education, science and transport.

The modern metropolis is marked by impressive civic architecture, monuments, squares and parks that demonstrate a great deal of pride in the city. The parks are particularly impressive and it is well worth joining the locals for an evening stroll or weekend picnic.

The story of this pride can be seen in the area's museums which tell of everything from the region's earliest archaeological findings to its first 4WD vehicles and its first appearance as an international air transport hub.

Discovery Centre
06 558 6577

Nr Sharjah International Airport   www.discoverycentre.ae

The Discovery Centre offers a great family day out and children of all ages, including toddlers, can explore the many themed areas and experiment and interact with the exhibits. The underlying aim is to teach youngsters about the biological, physical and technological worlds in a practical way. There is good pushchair access, an in-house cafe serving a light menu and ample parking. Entrance is Dhs.5 for children and Dhs.10 for adults. Open from 08:00 to 14:00 Sunday to Thursday, and 16:00 to 20:00 Friday and Saturday. Be aware it can get busy on the weekends. **Map** 5 P7

Al Mahatta Museum

Nr Al Estiqal St

06 573 3079
www.sharjahmuseums.ae

Home to the first airfield in the Gulf, from 1932 Sharjah played an important role as a primary stop-off point for the first commercial flights from Britain to India. The museum looks at the impact this had on the traditional way of life in Sharjah. There is some incredible film footage of the first flights arriving in the basic Bedouin settlement with passengers from Croydon decked out in their full furs and finery. Four of the original propeller planes have been fully restored and are on display. Entry is Dhs.5 for adults and Dhs.10 for families.
Map 1 E2

Parks

There are small parks in every residential area, over 30 throughout the city, and huge destination parks that are attractions in their own right. They are all popular with families, particularly at weekends, and there are always plenty of people out for a stroll, a game or a picnic. All the parks are well equipped with lawns, play areas and shaded seating. Picnics are encouraged and some have full barbecue facilities.

They typically open from 16:00 to 22:00, although many have ladies-only evenings and some are closed for much of the working week. There are very good signs at each gate listing all necessary information, rules and regulations in English and Arabic. Green Belt Park, just off Cultural Square, is a beautiful large park for ladies and children only. The largest is Sharjah National Park near the airport which is great for a whole day out with the family.

Sharjah Archaeology Museum

06 566 5466
Nr Cultural Square
www.sharjahmuseums.ae

This hi-tech museum offers an interesting display of antiquities from the region. Using well-designed displays and documentary film, the museum traces man's first steps and progress across the Arabian Peninsula through the ages. The results of archaeological excavations throughout Sharjah and the UAE are on display and serve to bring the past landscape and history to life. **Map** 1 G4

Sharjah Classic Car Museum

Nr Sharjah International Airport, Al Dhaid Road

The impressive collection of classic cars here changes as it is also a busy club. Mechanics can be seen working on restoring members' cars and there are always some incredible automobiles on show. **Map** 5 P7

Sharjah Police Museum

06 563 3333
Nr Al Zahra Square

Open by appointment only, the Police Museum is a fascinating insight into the origins of modern Sharjah. Original police equipment, including the first uniform and police car, can be seen. There is a full array of weaponry and kit as well as criminal artefacts and a series of awards. A model of the old forts and wall show just how far policing here has come from its watchtower origins.
Map 1 G2

Sharjah Science Museum
Nr Cultural Square

06 566 8777
www.sharjahmuseums.ae

One of the most popular museums in the region, its interactive exhibits and demonstrations cover subjects as diverse as aerodynamics, cryogenics, electricity and colour; and all in a fun, informative way. There is also a planetarium and children's area where the under 5s and their parents can learn together. The Learning Centre offers more in-depth programmes on many of the subjects covered in the museum. Entry is Dhs.5 for children and Dhs.10 for adults
Map 1 G4

Dr. Sultan Al Qassimi Centre Of Gulf Studies
University City

With a number of exhibits and resources from His Highness' private collection this is an intellectual hub of regional Gulf studies. There is a comprehensive archive library and displays of historical documents, maps, models and coins.

University City
Nr Sharjah International Airport, south of Al Dhaid Road

An impressive architectural complex, this grand destination illustrates the proud standards of educational excellence through brick and marble. It is well worth a drive around the buildings to get a feel for this centre of learning, and there are a number of lively student cafes and eateries just outside the gates of the complex. **Map** 5 M6

If you only do one thing in...
The City

Head to Al Mahatta Museum, the region's first airfield, and you will realise when you leave that you drove in on the original runway. The videos of the early passengers arriving en route to India are hilarious.

Best for...

Culture: The Archaeology Museum displays some extraordinary artefacts that make the story of early settlements in the area come to life.

Eating: Join the busy student crowd in the many eateries surrounding University City for a quick, tasty and good value snack.

Families: The Discovery Centre is a fantastic attraction for kids who find it great fun, even though they are being educated at the same time as being entertained.

Outdoor: Sharjah National Park is vast, beautifully landscaped and perfect for a weekend barbecue picnic and outdoor games.

Fun and learning in Sharjah

Out Of The City

Sharjah's hinterland is a major attraction with incredible natural history destinations to enjoy and amazing landscapes to explore.

Starting on the outskirts of the city, the impressive Sharjah desert appeals to visitors who are drawn by its startling beauty and vast emptiness. Hidden amongst the sands are the fantastic wildlife attractions of the Arabian Wildlife Centre, for marvelling at the Arabian leopards and other indigenous creatures, and for enjoying the tamer wildlife of the Children's Farm and Animal Sanctuary. The landscape itself is a wild attraction well worth exploring as are the towns of Al Dhaid and Al Madam.

Animal Sanctuary & Petting Farm
050 273 0973
4km SE of Exit 84, E611   www.poshpawsdubai.com

Popular with families and children of all ages, this friendly farm is indeed a sanctuary. Rescued animals live the good life here and visitors are encouraged to enjoy hands-on interaction with the horses, goats, rabbits, parrots and even one baby baboon. Open every day from 10:00 to 17:00.

Archaeological Sites

Throughout Sharjah are sites dating from the Iron Age with rich evidence of a number of villages from around 1000-500BC which suggests the existence of a large, agriculturally-

based population which tapped the rich underground aquifers of the Hajar mountains by means of falaj irrigation technology. Excavations have even revealed the existence of large, prehistoric graves dating to circa 3000BC.

The latest burials, of a man holding an iron spear and accompanied by a camel, date to the very end of the pre-Islamic era or the first century of Islam. Detailed findings can be seen at the Sharjah Archaeology Museum (p.86), which can also advise on visiting the sites.

Al Awadi Field Study Centre

050 398 9354

10km west of Dhaid

www.ecoventureme.com

The first dedicated field studies and sustainable development centre in the Middle East, this is an impressive new development. The professional setup is geared to get the best out of visiting students and bring their studies to life through scientific studies and outdoor activities. Groups can hire the campsite and Ecoventures can also arrange adventure camps and tours in the area.

Big Red

West of Madam, on the E44 Hatta Rd

One of the most famous dunes in the region, Big Red is exactly that: a big, red dune. It is a great favourite of off-roaders for its size and the scope of adventures around it. There are a couple of places along the road to hire quad bikes or motorbikes; it is also possible to take your own 4x4 onto the dunes nearby, though be sure to always have at least one other vehicle with you.

Al Dhaid

An important oasis town, Al Dhaid is the heart of Sharjah's hinterland. It lies east of Sharjah city, on the other side of the great expanse of rolling sand dunes at the point before the Hajar mountains rise high beyond, where the sand gives up to gravel plains. There is water here as evidenced by the many palm groves and farmsteads that surround the town.

The shopping is good with freshly picked fruit and vegetables (the strawberries are world-famous), and a wide selection of toys, carpets, pots and plants. There is a Sharjah Co-op and an Al Safer Hypermarket as well as many independent stores. Banks, supermarkets, and sweet and honey shops join the many tent makers, carpenters, metalworkers and mechanics. There is a camel race track nearby and the Dhaid Cricket Village is an important contributor to the growth of the sport in this region.

Fossil Rock

West of Dhaid, off the S116 Sharjah-Kalba Road

Nowhere is more spectacular, or better for finding fossils at than the appropriately named Fossil Rock. Also known as Jebel Maleihah this near-400m monolith rises out of the surrounding sands like an enormous natural monument. Clearly visible from over 25km away, Fossil Rock is a famous landmark and a key destination for off-road enthusiasts. The surrounding dunes provide plenty of opportunities for the adventurous with terrain to suit all levels of skill and ability.

Fossil Rock

Al Hamriyah

This enclave to the north of Sharjah city and the neighbouring emirate of Ajman is famed for its port and free zone. Business is booming here and soon luxury waterfront living will arrive when the Nuroom Island development opens. In the meantime the fishing harbour, market and beach make for an interesting picnic option.

Al Hashmia Date Farm   06 574 8888
East of Dhaid

This date farm and factory is a fascinating place to stop at on the road from Dhaid to the east coast. Busiest during the June to September harvest, you can nevertheless enjoy a guided

tour all year round and see the full progress of dates from young palms, through maturing, harvesting, stoning and storing; and of course you can taste and take away the most delicious dates you'll have ever tried.

Al Madam

The southernmost town of the Sharjah hinterland, Al Madam is a busy farming, trading and crossroads community. There are great value shops here for everything from locally grown fruit and vegetables, souvenirs, toys; even motorbikes and 4x4s. The expert carpentry, metalwork and mechanic workshops can assist with almost any project.

Sharjah Desert Park   06 531 1411
Sharjah-Dhaid Rd
Entry to all of Desert Park is Dhs.15 for adults, free for children under 12. Open from 09:00 (14:00 Fridays, 11:00 Saturdays) to 17:30. Closed on Tuesdays.

Arabian Wildlife Centre
& Children's Farm   06 531 1411
Sharjah Desert Park
One of the region's great wildlife highlights, the centre is home to some of the last Arabian Leopards on the planet, which are critically endangered in the wild. The adjoining (but closed to the public) breeding centre is at the forefront of the conservation movement for this rarest of big cats. There are other attractions too, with a reptile and insect house, a birds section with a huge indoor aviary, a nocturnal

section and large outdoor enclosures for flamingos, mountain goats, Arabian oryx and cheetahs, which are now extinct in Arabia but were once abundant.

For an even more hands-on experience for the kids, farm animals can be petted at the Children's Farm where there are also picnic areas and cafes.

Natural History & Botanical Museums

06 531 1411
www.sharjahmuseums.ae

Sharjah Desert Park

The full story of Sharjah's role in the planet's natural history is told in these two adjoining museums. A series of inviting and intriguing spaces immerse the visitor in displays that go right back to the age of dinosaurs and beyond. Meteorites, fossils, model volcanoes and action-posed dinosaur skeletons illustrate the history.

At the Botanical Museum, plants are celebrated for the role they have played in the development of human civilization with demonstrations of their diversity of uses, from building materials to foodstuffs. The displays and information boards are very well laid out, and a visit here will make you look differently at all plants, particularly desert plants.

Sharjah Monument

Sharjah-Dhaid Rd, Nr Sharjah Desert Park

From far afield the great, 28m high monolith monument can be seen on top of its hill. Commemorating Sharjah's role as the Arab culture capital for 1998, it depicts a huge arrow pointing skywards.

If you only do one thing in...
Out Of The City

Head to the Arabian Wildlife Centre to see the region's indigenous wildlife and then take an exciting off-roading trip to get a feel for the habitat.

Best for...

Culture: A day out at the Sharjah Desert Park will encourage an appreciation of the incredible achievements of man, beast and plant in colonising this region.

Eating: Head to Dhaid and pick up a picnic of the freshest local produce to enjoy on top of a dune in the middle of the desert, an unbeatable setting.

Families: The Animal Sanctuary & Petting Farm is a popular, fun and friendly place to get close to an extraordinary array of animals.

Outdoor: The wild landscape is a world-class attraction in its own right and an off-road trip is essential for all visitors to the region; don't miss the remarkable Fossil Rock.

Clockwise from top: dawn in the desert, flamingos at the Arabian Wildlife Park, afternoon in a wadi

The East Coast

The east coast is absolutely idyllic, an undiscovered land of rugged mountains overlooking golden beaches and clear blue seas.

On the shores of the Gulf of Oman, you'll find a peaceful retreat, far removed from the hustle and bustle of the city, yet accessible in under two hours' drive from Sharjah city. Your journey east will pass through the rugged scenery of the Hajar Mountains and bring you down to the clear blue waters that wash the shores of the seaside towns of Dibba Al Hisn, Khor Fakkan and Kalba. Although this spectacular coast can be visited in a day, it is best experienced with an overnight stay in the Oceanic Hotel, Breeze Motel (www.breezemotel.com) or, for the more adventurous, in a tent on the beach.

Beaches

At the southernmost stretch of the UAE, the Gulf of Oman is an alluring green-blue sea lapping against cinnamon sands. The long, chocolate ice cream coloured beach at Khor Kalba is a quiet and remote spot where you can drive right onto the beach and literally roll out of the car door into the sea. Just to the north, the beach in Kalba has a lighter coloured sand and is often busy with footballers, picnickers and fishermen and their Toyota trucks. At Khor Fakkan the long crescent beach is a hive of activity with all kinds of activity and entertainment available.

Diving

Underwater the east coast is incredible. From seahorses to whale sharks, turtles to manta rays, a kaleidoscope of corals and fascinating wrecks make the waters here amongst the best in Arabia for diving and snorkelling. There is an amazing array of well-researched dive sites and very well-respected operators to take you out. Shark Island (just off Khor Fakkan), Martini Rock and Snoopy Island all offer a good chance of seeing headline marine life and are well worth exploring.

Dibba Al Hisn

The most northerly of the east coast towns, Dibba Al Hisn is today a beautiful and well-to-do town with impressive mosques, immaculate villas, a huge cultural centre and public library, and a strong community feel. Famous in Islamic history as the site of one of the great battles of the Ridda wars, Dibba incorporates three separate entities: Dibba Al Hisn is owned by Sharjah, Dibba Muhallab belongs to Fujairah and Dibba Bayah is owned by the Sultanate of Oman. Sharjah's town is notably well groomed and hosts the two Omani border posts, the fishing harbour and port and the fort. **Map** 2 B5

Dibba Al Hisn Eating

The fishing market is proud of its impressive catch and the little cafeteria inside the market is a good option for a simple meal. To linger a while longer over your meal, join the locals for grilled fish and afternoons of tea and conversation at Bayota restaurant, near the fort, overlooking the port.

Dibba Al Hisn Exploring

Fishing boats and dhows can be chartered for short trips. Dolphins are often sighted and the boats can take you to deserted coves and some superb snorkelling spots. The Omani stretch of beach by the mountains is a popular spot for camping. The fort at Dibba Al Hisn is worth a visit to appreciate its importance as one of a series of coastal strongholds and lookouts.

Dibba Al Hisn Shopping

The covered souk is a great place to buy all kinds of souvenirs, toys, textiles, clothes and household goods. It is near the fort, one block in from the corniche on the parallel street. The same street also has bicycle shop. Many more shops can be found on the main strip, including a Sharjah Co-op.

Kalba

Kalba is a magical place. It is an impressive town with fantastic municipal facilities, parks and residential areas. There are endless stretches of beach, a vibrant fishing community, great shopping options, fantastic places to eat, fascinating and ancient history, and incredible geography including a unique habitat for some of the world's most endangered creatures.

All along the beaches and on every spare strip of land there are impromptu football pitches and the local team has made it into the UAE's top football league. With the natural attractions, the beaches and the football, Kalba is a little Rio De Janeiro on the Gulf of Oman. **Map** 4

Exploring the east coast by boat

Kalba Activities

The beaches are perfect for football matches (there is always a game to join), volleyball, picnics or even camping down on the quiet Khor Kalba beach. There are quadcycles for hire on the corniche surrounding the mangroves, at the Sheikh Saeed Al Qassimi Street roundabout on the northern end of the mangrove lagoon. There is a car hire office on the northernmost shopping stretch and moped hire can be arranged from Fujairah. You can see top class football at the Al Ittihad Kalba stadium; take the children to a playground or heritage area; or even kayak with turtles and kingfishers in the mangroves.

Kalba Creek (Khor Kalba)

Just a few kilometres south of Kalba town, this tidal creek (khor) is the site of Arabia's oldest mangrove forest and is a crucial conservation area for endangered species. The mangrove is inhabited by two of the world's rarest birds: the white-collared kingfisher and Syke's Warbler. Both species can be seen reasonably regularly, the warbler a busy little bundle of dark and sandy brown, the kingfisher a flash of turquoise plumage.

The dark, green mangroves provide a beautiful contrast to the purple-tinged, rocky Hajar Mountains and shimmering, clear, blue waters of the creek. The waters are also an important feeding ground for turtles who swim right up the creek and can often be seen from the banks or even the main bridge; but this teeming ecosystem is best appreciated by kayak; see p.130. **Map** 4 H6

Kalba Eating

The best restaurant for miles around is the Beit Al Nokhetha Restaurant just south of the fishing harbour which has been known to draw diners from the other side of the country for its sublimely grilled fresh fish, delicious Lebanese accompaniments and tables-on-the-beach setting.

The Breeze Grill also has an awesome setting, overlooking the mouth of the creek so that you can watch the fishermen coming in and turtles bobbing by while enjoying the fine cuisine.

Just north of the Breeze Motel, at the fishermen's launching area, is a fantastically simple cafe with unbeatably fresh fish and an authentic atmosphere, as evidenced by the old fishermen drinking tea under the old tree. There is more fantastically fresh fish at the fishmarket. Those with a sweet tooth shouldn't miss Al Kashmir Honey & Dates.

Kalba Shopping

Kalba Shopping Centre, Al Safeer Centre and the Sharjah Co-op are ideal for all essentials. There is a fantastic market opposite the Al Safeer Centre which sells huge footballs, inflatable penguins, assorted toys and all the barbecue, kitchen and camping paraphernalia that any beach party could ever need. The main streets are busy with florists, bookshops, pharmacies, tailors, hairdressers and banks.

Kalba Fort, Al Hisn   09 277 4442

For forts in this landscape, it is all about the view. Just set back from the sea, on the other side of the road from the Al

Qassimi House, Kalba Fort stands on a raised platform with clear, wide-ranging views out to sea and back across the plains to the Hajar mountains and the Al Hayl Fort. Together, the forts in the area provided a comprehensive security and communication system. A trip around these forts will give a real insight into their history. Here there are weapons and artefacts inside and cannons and seesaws outside – and then there are the views. Entrance is Dhs.3 for individuals and Dhs.6 for families. **Map** 4 H1

Kalba Museum, Al Qassimi House
Right on the seafront, just north of the fishing harbour, this house was built at the end of the 19th century and belonged to His Highness Sheikh Saeed Bin Hamed Al Qassimi, a former ruler of Sharjah. The different rooms give a good insight into ways of life a century ago. Old photographs, coins, artefacts and poetry assist in creating an intriguing atmosphere.

Open from 09:00 to 13:00 (Saturday-Thursday) and 17:00 to 20:00 (Friday-Thursday), closed on Mondays. Dhs.3 for adults, Dhs.6 for families. **Map** 4 H1

Khor Fakkan
The name Khor Fakkan translates as 'Creek of the Two Jaws,' reflecting its setting in a splendid bay flanked on either side by two headlands. This is Sharjah's largest town on the east coast, found halfway between Kalba and Dibba Al Hisn. It is a prosperous and impressive settlement. On the approach from the south you pass the immaculate University of Sharjah campus cluttered in folds of the Hajar mountains. There is

Kayaking at Khor Kalba

a sizeable community of large villas and blocks of flats, a comprehensive industrial area in the south and a good deal of shopping and entertainment options.

There is still evidence of the fresh water wells that still keep palm groves and other crops lush today. Fresh water and such impressive geography mean that the bay has a long history; graves and other evidence suggesting a settlement from more than 3,000 years ago have been found on rocky outcrops overlooking the bay.

The bay today is home to a busy commercial port at the southern end (also home to a fantastic fish, fruit and vegetable market), with the Oceanic Hotel at the northern end. In between the curving corniche is a busy parade of shops, cafeterias, play areas and long crescent beach. A mountainous hillock, crowned with a royal palace, rises high over the corniche. **Map** 3

Khor Fakkan Activities

There is a whole holiday's worth of activities on offer all along the corniche, as well as in hills above and waters below. There are seven jetski hire huts at about the midway point of the corniche (050 271 3366, 050 780 7999, 050 662 8626). Among the palm trees on the beach are swings, volleyball nets and football goals.

The Oceanic Hotel (www.oceanichotel.com) offers a full range of watersports, diving, fishing and boating activities. Behind the hotel is a lovely park with a little train. Another park to the north has a staircase up through the cliffs to give views to the hidden cove below. Fishing

trips are highly recommended and the Oceanic Hotel can arrange everything.

Khor Fakkan Eating
The Oceanic Hotel has a rooftop restaurant and beachside cafe. There are a couple of good Lebanese restaurants and a series of near-identical cafeterias right on the beach which are a good option for an alfresco snack. The fish market at the southern end of the bay is sparklingly clean and has an excellent little cafe. The nearby Marbella Cafe is famed for its donuts, while inland there are also plenty of cafeterias.

Khor Fakkan Exploring
Shark Island lies just out in the bay and despite the name is a charming and unthreatening place for snorkelling, camping and picnics. Directly inland from town, Rifaisa Dam lies amid the mountains and legend has it that when the water is clear a lost village can be seen at the bottom of the reservoir. Right on the corniche, towards the fishing harbour, the heritage area is a traditionally-styled compound right on the beach with an exhibition dhow, stalls, a stage and frequent impressive heritage shows.

Nahwa Enclave
This is an absolutely unique curiosity. The village of Nahwa is a little enclave of Sharjah, within an enclave of Oman, within an enclave of Dubai, within the UAE. It is worth a visit just to admire the municipal pride and friendliness of this small pocket of Sharjah.

Exploring

If you only do one thing in...
The East Coast

Complete the East coast roadtrip, stopping in each of the towns, exploring the Khor Kalba mangroves, swimming off the beach there and finishing in one of the fantastic Kalba restaurants.

Best for...

Culture: The fort at Dibba Al Hisn is a fascinating insight into the area's history.

Eating: Kalba is the place to eat, and the Beit Al Nokhetha Restaurant in particular. Its grilled fish and beach setting are highly regarded.

Outdoor: It would be ridiculous to not explore the underwater east coast. It really is an aquarium world out there and easily accessible to snorkellers and divers alike, particularly from Khor Fakkan.

Sightseeing: A kayak trip through the Khor Fakkan mangroves is an essential, world-class tourist experience – and you might even spot one of the incredibly rare white-collared kingfishers.

Views of the east coast

Further Out

Beyond Sharjah, the UAE has spectacular sights and experiences, from modern cities to ancient forts, exciting events to desert wilderness.

Of the six other emirates which make up the UAE, Abu Dhabi, Dubai, Ajman, Umm Al Quwain and Ras Al Khaimah lie on the west coast, and Fujairah on the east coast. Each of the emirates has its own distinct character: Abu Dhabi is the fast-growing capital, Dubai is a glitzy tourist hotspot, and Fujairah is home to breathtakingly beautiful landscapes. If your stay is long enough to permit exploration of the other emirates, you should definitely make the effort to experience their unique characteristics.

Abu Dhabi

The capital of the UAE today accounts for 10% of the world's known crude oil reserves, making it the richest emirate. It is home to numerous internationally renowned hotels, a selection of shiny shopping malls and a sprinkling of culture in the form of heritage sites and souks. The malls are much less busy than in Dubai and goods are sometimes cheaper.

Travellers to the city shouldn't miss the Sheikh Zayed Grand Mosque (800 555, www.visitabudhabi.ae). The mosque covers 22,000 sqm and is the sixth-largest in the world. During the cooler months, the blue tile-covered corniche on the gulf-side of the city is a great place for an evening

stroll. Abu Dhabi has big plans to build up its international appeal as a tourist destination; Formula 1 took place in the country for the first time in 2009, and both the Louvre and Guggenheim museums are being brought to town in the near future.

Outside the city, Abu Dhabi emirate is home to the oasis towns of Al Ain and Liwa. Al Ain is Abu Dhabi's second city and certainly worthy of a visit. South-west of Abu Dhabi is the Liwa oasis, where the spectacular dunes are a photographer's dream. Liwa lies at the edge of the Rub Al Khali (Empty Quarter), one of the largest sand deserts in the world.

Dubai

Dubai is the place that the whole world is talking about. Although the breakneck speed of construction has slowed due to the global recession, it is still a fascinating city to visit. Among the high-rises you'll find the tallest building in the world, the Burj Khalifa, a selection of the world's most luxurious hotels, some amazing leisure facilities (an indoor ski slope with real snow, to name just one), designer hotels, celebrity-chef endorsed restaurants and several stunning beaches.

There are also a number of world renowned events worth checking out. Renowned as the 'shopping capital of the Middle East', Dubai is the ultimate place for a shopaholic with a healthy credit limit. The enormous Ibn Battuta Mall, Mall of the Emirates (the one with the ski slope) and the record-breaking The Dubai Mall are all easily accessible from Sheikh Zayed Road, the main highway south from Sharjah.

Fujairah

Fujairah is the youngest of the seven emirates. Overlooking the atmospheric old town is a fort that is reportedly about 300 years old. The surrounding hillsides are dotted with more such ancient forts and watchtowers, which add an air of mystery and charm. The site of the oldest mosque in the UAE, Bidiyah, is roughly half way down the East Coast, north of Khor Fakkan. The building is believed to date back to the middle of the 15th century and was restored in 2003. The village is considered one of the oldest settlements on the East Coast, which is thought to have been inhabited since 3000BC.

Northern Emirates

North of Sharjah are Ajman, Umm Al Quwain and Ras Al Khaimah. These emirates are smaller in size than Sharjah and are also less developed. Ajman is the smallest of the emirates, but its proximity to Sharjah has enabled it to grow considerably. It has one of the largest dhow building centres in the region, offering a chance to see these massive wooden boats being built with rudimentary tools using skills passed down through the generations. Ajman also has some great beaches and a pleasant corniche. Much of the nightlife revolves around the Ajman Kempinski Hotel & Resort (06 714 5555, www.ajmankempinski.com).

Umm Al Quwain has the smallest population and little has changed over the years, though it is home to the expansive Dreamland Aqua Park (www.dreamlanduae.com). Two of the most interesting activities Umm Al Quwain has to offer are

crab hunting and mangrove tours; the Flamingo Beach Resort (06 765 0000; www.flamingoresort.ae) offers both.

Ras Al Khaimah (RAK) is the most northerly of the seven emirates but you can make the trip from Sharjah in under an hour. With the jagged Hajar Mountains rising just behind the city, and the Arabian Gulf stretching out from the shore, RAK has some of the best scenery in the UAE. A creek divides the city into the old town and the newer Al Nakheel district. For a day trip, you should go the souk in the old town and the National Museum of Ras Al Khaimah (07 233 3411). From there you can explore the surrounding countryside and visit the ancient sites of Ghalilah and Shimal.

Oman

Just a few hours from Sharjah, you'll find the countless attractions of Oman. It's a peaceful and breathtaking country, with history, culture and spectacular scenery. The capital, Muscat, has enough attractions to keep you busy for a short break, including beautiful beaches, some great restaurants and cafes, and the mesmerising old souk at Mutrah. Out of the capital you will find many historic old towns and forts, and some of the most stunning mountain and wadi scenery in the region. Salalah, in the south, has the added bonus of being cool and wet in the summer. Isolated from the rest of the country, on the tip of the Arabian Peninsula, is the Omani enclave of Musandam. With its jagged mountains and fjord-like inlets, it is a must-visit if you are in Sharjah for any serious length of time. For further information see the *Oman Mini Visitors' Guide*.

Tours & Sightseeing

Whether by boat, bus or 4WD an organised tour is a hassle-free way of maximising your sightseeing time and experiencing a different side to the UAE.

An organised tour can be a great way of discovering Sharjah, especially if you're only here for a short time. Whether you prefer activities, sightseeing or shopping, you'll find a tour to suit you. The majority of tours need to be booked in advance and most tour operators visit the main hotels in order to book tours for guests. Some trips may need to be arranged further in advance, especially if they involve travel to another emirate. Hotel concierges should have information on which tours are available and when, and may even be able to get you a special deal.

Tours & Sightseeing

Abu Al Hoal Tourism	06 574 3374
Al Buhaira Travel Agency	06 561 4593
Al Faisal Travel & Tourism Agency	06 568 3333
Al Khalidiah Tours	06 528 6057
Al Wahda Travels	06 533 0477
Arabian Link Tours	06 572 6666
Arabian Travel Agency	06 561 0000
Cordial Tours & Cargo	06 572 5142
DNATA	06 569 2300
Elaf Tourism	06 564 1010
Intercontinental Travel	06 569 1448
Kanoo Travel	06 561 6058
Orient Tours	800 6789
Orient Travel & Touring Agency	06 568 3838
Planet Travel Tours & Cargo	06 558 1401
Sharaf Travels	06 569 4000
Sharjah Airport Travel Agency (SATA)	06 561 8888
Sharjah National Travel and Tourist Agency (SNTTA)	06 568 4411
South East Asia Tours	06 559 7881
Syrian Tourism Centre	06 559 7722
Travel & Marketing Services	06 557 0630
Tropic International Tours	06 574 5959
Victoria Travel Agency	06 561 7444

Tours & Sightseeing

The beach at Khor Fakkan

Sports & Spas

Active Sharjah

From the west coast to the east, there's so much to explore no matter whether you want to be active, adventurous or just kick back and relax.

It's not just the heritage that attracts visitors to Sharjah. It is the only emirate with territory on both coasts, so you can swim from a city beach, hike through the mountains, dive in the Indian Ocean and kayak through the world's most northerly mangrove forest, all without leaving Sharjah.

Sharjah is a great adventure sport destination, from off-roading (p.126) to diving (p.130); adrenaline junkies are well catered for. If you prefer ball sports to extreme sports, you won't be disappointed; from the UAE's original rugby club (p.128) to one of its newest golf courses (p.124), Sharjah has it all. And, when the weather heats up, keep cool at the emirate's ice rinks (p.126) and bowling alleys (p.122). Fancy yourself as a sure shot? Make the most of Sharjah's top class archery (p.120) and shooting ranges (p.128).

Watersports (p.130) fans are in for a treat. Kayak trips of the Khor Kalba mangroves (p.102) are exercise, nature and education all rolled into one. World championship powerboat races (p.134) are exciting spectacles. And traditional Arabian sports such as camel racing (p.132) shouldn't be missed.

All this activity aside, those who view a holiday as a chance for relaxation will find a collection of spas and beauty salons where top treatments are surprisingly reasonably priced.

Activities in Sharjah

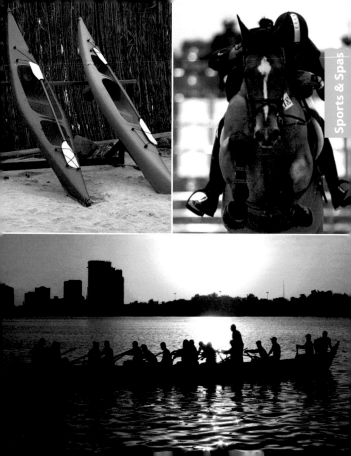

With kilometre upon kilometre of coast, mountain and desert, the possibilities for action-packed adventure are endless.

Sports & Activities

Archery

Dubai Archers

Samnan

06 558 6239
www.sharjahwanderers.com

Now hosted by Sharjah Wanderers, as the name suggests this club originated in neighbouring Dubai. The club has two target ranges, one for beginners and intermediate archers (10m, 20m and 30m) and the other for experienced and advanced archers (50m, 70m and 90m). A state-of-the-art 3D range with up to six plastic animal targets should be available soon.

Shooting sessions are held on Fridays from 10:00 to 12:00; more sessions may be added depending on demand. The club hosts an annual competition at the end of January or beginning of February which is open to all.

Beginners can book tuition and equipment hire, for Dhs.60 per session, for four sessions before having to apply for associate membership of Sharjah Wanderers; experienced archers must apply for associate membership. Private tuition costs Dhs.100 per hour. The Sharjah Wanderers Club has fantastic facilities and a friendly atmosphere, with visitors and new members always welcomed.

Sharjah Golf & Shooting Club

Sharjah Golf & Shooting Club

06 548 7777

Emirates Road

www.golfandshootingshj.com

Target archery, using state of the art equipment, is offered at the indoor 20 yard range at SGSC. Tuition is available for all levels from qualified trainers and competitions are held throughout the year. The range is open Saturday to Thursday from 12:00 to 22:00 and from 14:00 to 22:00 on Fridays, with sessions costing from Dhs.60 to Dhs.70 (round only) for Dhs.80 to Dhs.90 (lesson and round).

Bowling

A great indoor activity for the long hot days of summer.

Ewan Bowling Centre   06 528 0111
Ewan Hotel

Open daily from 09:00 to 02:00; Dhs.10 per person or Dhs.70 per lane, per hour (includes shoe rental). (10 lanes)

Radisson Blu Resort   06 565 7777
Radisson Blu Hotel

Open daily 13:00 to 22:00; Dhs.15 per person, per game (Dhs.5 extra for shoe hire). (6 lanes)

Sky 24   06 556 0005
Al Durrah Tower, Khalid Lagoon

Bowling on the 24th floor. Open Saturday to Thursday 10:00 to 22:00 and 14:00 to 22:00 on Fridays; Dhs.15 per person, per game or Dhs.80 per lane for an hour (includes shoe rental). (3 lanes)

Cricket

Second only to football in popularity, impromptu cricket matches can be found on most areas of wasteland on Fridays and during the evenings.

Sharjah is also home to the 27,000 capacity Sharjah Cricket Association Stadium which, between 1984 and 2003, hosted One Day International tournaments involving the world's top teams. The stadium has been designated as the home ground for Afghanistan's national cricket team for all One Day

Internationals and first class matches; they also have full use of the facilities at Al Dhaid Cricket Village.

Al Dhaid Cricket Village is a 10,000 capacity venue used by international teams for training and as the host of local competitions including the Al Dhaid Ramadan Cup. Sharjah Cricket Stadium also played host to the Bangladesh Twenty20 League in 2010.

Contact the Sharjah Cricket Council (06 532 2991) or Sharjah Cricket Club (06 543 3154) for details on upcoming fixtures and for more information on the sport.

There is also cricket coaching available at the Verona Resort (06 522 8820, www.veronaresort-sharjah.com).

Dhow Cruises

There are many operators who offer cruises on the east coast, sailing north from Dibba to explore the Musandam peninsula. Trips take you along the coastline where steep rocky cliffs rise out of the sea. You'll pass small fishing villages and will perhaps see dolphins and turtles, and have the chance to snorkel in the pristine waters.

Prices start at around Dhs.200 per adult for a full day, including lunch, refreshments and snorkelling gear. Cruises depart from the Omani side of Dibba (see p.99) and can be arranged by most hotels or tour operators.

Dhow cruises also operate around Khalid Lagoon (p.71) and offer a great opportunity to view the modern city from the form of transport that first defined it and brought it fame and wealth. These cruises can be organised by hotels and tour operators or just joined as you wander along the corniche.

Football

The 'beautiful game' is as popular in Sharjah as it is across the rest of the planet. If you're in need of an organised game while you're in Sharjah, head for Sharjah Wanderers (www.sharjahwanderers.com). Impromptu games happen in parks and on beaches throughout the emirate, particularly at Kalba on the east coast (p.100), and visitors are often welcomed as extra players.

Golf

Sharjah Golf & Shooting Club

06 548 7777

Emirates Road   www.golfandshootingshj.com

Boasting a fully floodlit, Peter Harradine designed 9 hole course, this is Sharjah's first fully grassed course. Played twice, the course is a par 72 in excess of 7,300 yards, and with between five and seven tee positions on each hole, it offers considerable variety and interest; and that's before you negotiate the water hazards and bunkers.

The Academy's facilities include a 300m fully grassed driving range, 6,425 square metre world class short game area and 1,095 square metre putting green; all of which are fully floodlit. The club is welcoming to members and guests of all levels, with PGA professionals on hand to offer expert tuition.

Coaching programmes are suitable for all ages, and equipment is available for hire. A 9 hole round costs from Dhs.120 (members) to Dhs.180, with 18 hole rounds costing from Dhs.175 (members) to Dhs.305.

Floodlit night golf

Sharjah Wanderers Golf Club

06 558 6239

Samnan

www.sharjahwanderers.com

A challenging 'links' course awaits members and guests at this well established Sharjah golf course. Making the best use of the natural topography, the course presents a challenge to both beginners and experienced players, as conditions change throughout the day. The course is a great example of the local golfing peculiarity where 'browns' are played rather than 'greens', though nine of the 18 fairways have so far been grassed and there are plans to continue this when possible.

Guests are permitted to play three rounds (Dhs.50 per 18 hole round) before they must apply for associate membership of Sharjah Wanderers; membership costs from Dhs.2,430 for an individual to Dhs.4,855 for a family.

Horse Riding

Sharjah Equestrian & Racing Club
06 531 1188
Out of the city
www.serc.ae

Established in 1982, SERC is one of the UAE's top equestrian facilities with one of the largest indoor riding facilities in the Middle East. The riding school is supervised by qualified international trainers and schooled horses are available for children and beginners. Pony tours are offered for young children and cost Dhs.20. Group lessons (1 hour) cost from Dhs.80.

Ice Skating

A great activity to get you out of the heat on a sweltering summer's day.

Sharjah Ladies Club
06 506 7822
North Corniche
www.slc.ae

Dhs.35 per hour for non-members with skate rental (boys must be under 9 years of age); tuition is available.

Sky 24
06 556 0005
Al Durrah Tower, Khalid Lagoon

Dhs.15 per hour inclusive of skate hire.

Off-Roading

Most car rental agencies offer visitors 4WDs capable of desert driving. If renting a 4WD, make sure you get the details of the insurance plan, as many rental insurers won't cover damage

caused by off-roading. Dune bashing, or desert driving, is one of the toughest challenges for both car and driver, but once you have mastered it it's a lot of fun.

If you do venture out into the desert, it is a good idea to have at least one experienced driver and one other car to help tow you out if you get stuck. Most major tour companies offer a range of desert and mountain safaris if you'd rather leave the driving to the professionals.

Driving in wadis is usually a bit more straightforward. Wadis are (usually) dry gullies, carved through the rock by rushing floodwaters, following the course of seasonal rivers. The main safety precaution to take when wadi bashing is to keep your eyes open for rare, but not impossible, thunderstorms developing. The wadis can fill up quickly and you will need to make your way to higher ground pretty fast to avoid flash floods. For further information and tips on off-road driving, check out the UAE Off-Road Explorer guidebook.

Paintballing

Sharjah Golf & Shooting Club
Emirates Road

06 548 7777
www.golfandshootingshj.com

The paintball park at SGSC is world famous and is among the very best in the Middle East. The extraordinary and exciting floodlit park can accommodate up to 150 players in one session in teams of up to 14 players. There are two phases: the 5,000 square metre jungle phase (complete with bunkers, trees, hills, trenches, bridges, hut and even an old aircraft) and the Sahara phase; you can also indulge in a spot of target

practise to help hone your skills. The park is run by friendly and qualified marshals and state of the art equipment is provided and for sale in the pro shop.

The park is open from 10:00 to 22:00 and refreshments and changing rooms are available.

Packages cost from Dhs.85 to Dhs.500 per person.

Rugby

Sharjah Wanderers Rugby Club

06 558 6239

Nr Cultural Square, Samnan

www.swrfc.com

The original home of rugby in the UAE, Sharjah Wanderers Rugby Football Club was founded in 1976. Based at Sharjah Wanderers, the club has active men's, ladies, veterans and junior sections and is always open to new members.

Shooting

Sharjah Ladies Club

06 506 7777

North Corniche

www.slc.ae

Established under the patronage of Her Highness Sheikha Jawaher bint Mohammad Al Qassimi, the 14 lanes are open to both air pistol and air rifle shooters. The facility has enabled the creation of a women's national shooting team. Instruction is available.

Sessions cost from Dhs.100 with a coach, to Dhs.650 for a special package of eight sessions. The club is a luxurious five-star setup on the coast near the Radisson Blu resort and is a haven of pampering as well as shooting.

Activities at the Sharjah Golf & Shooting Club

Sharjah Golf & Shooting Club

06 548 7777

Emirates Road   www.golfandshootingshj.com

Facilities include ranges for indoor pistols, rifles and revolvers and 25m and 50m German Technology ranges. Weapons range from specialised target pistols to .22 M16s. Safety is of paramount importance and a fully trained safety instructor accompanies visitors at all times. Instruction is available. Rounds (25 shots) start from Dhs.70 to Dhs.150 for members (without instruction) and from Dhs.90 to Dhs.200 for non-members (without instruction).

Watersports & Diving

Sharjah is unique among the emirates in having coast on both the Arabian Gulf and the Gulf of Oman, making it a dream destination for watersports lovers. The calm waters, sheltered coves and pristine beaches are ideal for getting out on the water and many of the beach hotels offer the opportunity to both guests and non-guests, although the latter may have to pay a beach fee. Many have equipment for sea kayaking, sailing and windsurfing, and some may offer waterskiing.

The fishing is good, particularly off the east coast, and many people come in search of big game fish as well as eating fish. The sport is superb, often fierce and frenetic, but at the end of it there is always a willing restaurant chef happy to barbecue your catch.

Kayaking is a wonderful way to get up close to nature and explore the coast and inshore waters. Weaving your way past the gnarled trunks and overhanging branches of the

mangrove forest, you may encounter turtles, crabs and even the critically endangered (there are only around 50 breeding pairs) Halcyon Chloris Kalbaensis, or white-collared kingfisher which is unique to this small area.

Diving is popular and the clear waters off the east coast are home to a variety of marine species, coral life and even shipwrecks. You'll see exotic fish, possibly moray eels, small sharks, barracuda, stingrays, sea snakes and even turtles. Another option for diving enthusiasts is a trip to Musandam. Part of the Sultanate of Oman (p.113), it is often described as the 'Norway of the Middle East' due to its many inlets and cliffs that plunge straight into the sea. Sheer wall dives with strong currents and clear waters are more suitable for advanced divers, while huge bays with calm waters and bountiful shallow reefs are ideal for the less experienced. Courses are offered under the usual international training organisations. More details on specific dives and sites can be found in the UAE Underwater Explorer guidebook.

Watersports & Diving

7 Seas Divers	09 238 7400	PADI Dive Centre
Chris Chellapermal	050 885 3238	PADI Instructor
Divers Down Centre	09 237 0299	PADI Dive Centre
Emirates Diving Centre	06 565 5990	PADI Dive Centre
Noukhada Adventure Company	050 721 8928	Kayak Hire & Tours
Sharjah Wanderers Dive Club	06 566 2105	BSAC Dive Centre
Sunset Fishing	09 238 5111	Fishing Charters

Spectator Sports

With top-class sporting action as well atmospheric local events, a sporting day out is a great way to get a feel for the emirate.

Camel Racing

This is a chance to see a truly traditional local sport, though now with a modern twist as the camels are steered by 'robot' jockeys, controlled by an operator in one of the gleaming 4WDs that follow the races. Races take place in the winter months and additional meetings are often held on public holidays. Races are usually held early on Thursday or Friday mornings (from 07:00, admission is free), but you should see camels out being exercised during the day in the cooler months. Sharjah's camel racecourse is near Al Dhaid, and there are tracks in each of the other emirates too.

Football

The UAE Football League is becoming big-time. Premier league clubs are investing heavily in players, coaches and infrastructure and the competition is going from strength to strength; 2010 even saw the arrival of Italian World Cup winning captain Fabio Cannavaro.

Sharjah has several clubs in Sharjah city as well as one in Dhaid, one in Dibba and Al Ittihad Club in Kalba (www.kalba-club.com). The little club from the east coast town of Kalba managed to make it into the top division in 2010 alongside

Showjumping in Sharjah

Sharjah's oldest club, Sharjah Sports Club (www.sharjahclub.ae), which won the first UAE football league in the 1973-1974 season and went on to supply the UAE national team with nine players for the 1990 FIFA World Cup. Matches are occasions of great atmosphere as well as great sport; see www.uaefa.com for fixture details.

Horse Racing & Showjumping

Sharjah Equestrian & Racing Club 06 531 1155
Out of the city   www.serc.ae

Horse racing in the UAE is great sport and big business, running from November all the way through to the world's

Spectator Sports

richest horserace, the Dubai World Cup, in late March. Sharjah holds meetings through the season, on Saturday afternoons, with six or seven races per meeting held at 30 minute intervals and the first race starting at about 14:00.

Entrance is free to all racecourses in the UAE and soft drinks and light snacks are available. A Pick Six competition to select the winners of each race is held at every meeting with big prizes on offer. Results of the competition are announced in the paddock following the final race. For more details of fixtures and timings see www.emiratesracing.com.

There are regular showjumping and dressage competitions throughout the season, from November to March. There is also a whole series of events for purebred Arabians. In Sharjah all related events are held at the equestrian and racing club, but there are also events across the UAE.

Powerboating

On the west coast, Sharjah's Khalid Lagoon plays host to the Sharjah Formula 1 Powerboat Grand Prix as part of the annual Sharjah Water Festival, held in December. Described as being akin to driving a Formula 1 car across a ploughed field, it is one of the most spectacular and exciting sports in the world and, as the season finale, Sharjah is its most dramatic home. The boats reach speeds of up to 225kph (130mph) as they race around the buoyed course. It is a high profile global event and is broadcast to 150 nations worldwide, while international visitors flock to Sharjah for the world-class sporting entertainment and accompanying attractions of the impressive Sharjah Water Festival.

Sharjah Formula 1 Powerboat Grand Prix

Spas

Take time out from all that exploring, sit back, relax and enjoy a spot of pampering at one of the city's many spas or beauty parlours.

A comprehensive range of treatments is on offer in the emirate, and you can find spas offering everything from ayurvedic treatments and mother to be packages to body peels, aromatherapy and traditional Middle Eastern hammams.

The price of treatments varies from spa to spa, and while manicures and pedicures can be cheap in the smaller spas and salons, you will pay a higher price at the top spas. Compare packages to get the best deal – and ask about their facilities as you will often be allowed to use their sauna, pool or Jacuzzi before or after your treatment.

Bay Club Spa
06 565 7777

Radisson Blu Hotel

Open to members and hotel guests, the spa is part of the Bay Club which provides comprehensive sports, fitness and leisure facilities. The serene spa offers a full range of expert massage services to rejuvenate body and mind. There are saunas and gyms with ladies-only options and temperature-controlled swimming pools for adults and children. There is also access to the private beach so that you can conclude your treatment relaxing in an oversized beach chair as the setting sun dips into the sea.

Relax in one of the many spas

Cleopatra's Boutique Spa

06 530 2222

Sharjah Golf & Shooting Club

These sophisticated urban spas provide a wide range of modern treatments including facials that cleanse, detoxify, rejuvenate and relax; and body treatments that retune, re-align and re-energize. The spa at the Golf and Shooting Club has separate areas for men and women, while over at the Sharjah Chamber of Commerce and Industry (06 530 2222) there is a new spa facility specifically designed as a contemporary relaxation space for men only.

Dalouk Spa
Sharjah Ladies Club

06 506 7777
www.slc.ae

Dalouk Spa offers Sharjah's most comprehensive spa menu, providing five-star luxury to members and guests. It is understandably one of the most popular spots for the fashionable ladies of Sharjah. Treatments include SunFX professional spray on tan, microdermabrasion facials, mesotherapy (the needle-free Botox alternative), the intriguing sounding 'Desert Journey' (a revitalising deep tissue massage), traditional hammam, balancing hot stone treatments and colour therapy. Other facilities include a Thalassotherapy pool.

Exotic Island Spa
Lou'Lou'a Beach Resort

06 528 5000

A full spa menu is on offer including massage therapies, body peels and wraps, facial treatments, aromatherapy, manicures and pedicures. The signature treatment is the 'Wild Orchid' aromatic full body massage which uses natural essences to moisturise and rejuvenate the skin.

Spa Ayurveda
The Oceanic Hotel

09 238 5111

Set in the grounds of The Oceanic Hotel, in the picturesque east coast town of Khor Fakkan, the spa's focus is on Ayurveda, the ancient Indian 'science of life'. It is a natural way to achieve health, harmony and happiness. A complete way of life, it uses diet, herbal medicines, gentle exercise and physical therapies to enhance health, longevity and vitality.

Hair & Beauty Salons

Salons can be found throughout Sharjah, from the hotels to the malls, and in many of the neighbourhoods. Most offer everything you could possibly need or desire from manicures, pedicures, facials, henna, waxing and threading, massage therapies and bridal packages, to haircuts, colouring and styling. Many places are very accomplished at manicures and pedicures, while the spas in the top hotels and at the Sharjah Ladies Club are the places to head to for truly indulgent pampering.

Orchid Beauty Boutique
Sharjah Ladies Club

06 506 7777
www.slc.ae

Five-star beauty treatments and services are offered at Orchid Beauty Boutique. A comprehensive range of facials, hair styling and colouring (including Kerastase treatments), makeup, manicures and pedicures, waxing and threading are available using leading professional brands.

Other Salons

Allure	06 522 2317	Shargan
Amouage	06 528 4888	Al Khan
Cosmesurge	06 524 5444	Al Rifa'ah
Elegance	06 574 8874	Al Qassimia
Jennifer	06 524 2688	Al Fisht
Moon Beauty	06 568 4502	Shuwaiheen
Philomena	06 572 7881	Al Majaz 1
Tips & Toes	06 556 0551	Al Fardan Centre

Shopping

Essentials

Contents

Welcome to the *Sharjah Mini Visitors' Guide*. This mini marvel has been passionately prepared so that you'll find all you need to make the most out of your time in this extraordinary emirate – from fascinating cultural spots and exciting attractions to the best places to eat, shop and adventure.

Sharjah is an incredible place, a modern metropolis with 6,000 years of history, an emirate with coastline on both the Arabian Gulf and the Gulf of Oman, a natural landscape that stretches from pristine undersea habitats to mangrove forests, sweeping sand deserts and tall craggy mountains. To find some of the region's most celebrated attractions and some of its most undiscovered gems, head to the **Exploring** chapter (p.64) for directions.

The **Pull-Out Map** at the back of the book will help with navigation, while **Essentials** (p.2) tells you all you need to plan a memorable trip. Turn to **Shopping** (p.140) for the best places for souvenirs, **Going Out** (p.162) for eating and entertainments and **Sports & Spas** (p.116) for all sorts of activities.

Happy exploring!

The Explorer Team

Welcome...

Shopping

With the traditional souks, independent shops and modern malls there's something to suit every pocket in Sharjah.

Sharjah is a dream destination for shoppers. Free of sales tax and boasting a fantastic range of international and traditional local items, temptation lies around every corner.

Mall culture is a comparatively new phenomenon in Sharjah where the main streets are lined with independent shops and major chains. Practicality plays a major part in the popularity of Sharjah's malls. During the hotter months the malls are oases of cool in the sweltering city – somewhere to eat, meet, shop and be entertained. And, with most shops open throughout the day and until at least 22:00 every night, there's plenty of time to browse. The popularity of the malls is evident from the crowds they pull, particularly at weekends, and it takes the most dedicated of shoppers to tackle them on a Friday evening.

Sharjah's souks (p.150) offer the UAE's most authentic shopping experience. Step back in time in the winding alleyways of Souk Al Arsah (p.152) and soak up the atmosphere while haggling over a carpet at the Central Souk (aka the Blue Souk) (p.150). A broad range of items are available in Sharjah's souks, and they're great places to try out your bargaining skills.

While prices for most items are comparable to elsewhere in the world, the frequent sales and wide range of outlets make it possible to find something to suit most budgets.

Sizing

Figuring out your size is pretty straightforward. International sizes are often printed on garment labels and the store will usually have a conversion chart on display. Otherwise, a UK size is two higher than a US size (so, a UK 10 is a US 6). To convert European sizes into US sizes, subtract 32 (so, a European 38 is a US 6). To convert European sizes into UK sizes, a 38 is roughly a 10. As for shoes, a women's UK 6 is a European 39 or US 8.5 and a men's UK 10 is a European 44 or a US 10.5. If in doubt, ask for help.

Bargaining

Bargaining is common in the souks and shopping areas of the UAE; you'll need to give it a go to get the best prices. When you've decided what to buy, try to get an idea of prices from a few different shops, as there can often be a significant difference, and set a top price limit. Your initial bid should be roughly half the amount that's being asked. Stay laidback and vaguely disinterested. When your initial offer is rejected (and it will be), keep going until you reach an

Bespoke Services

Good jewellers, tailors, carpenters and metalworkers will be able to make something to your own design, either from a photo or diagram, or by copying an existing item. It is essential to decide on the material, whether for a gold ring, new shirt or garden swing. A price should be agreed beforehand, and any alterations should be included in the fee, but payment should not be made until delivery.

agreement or until you have reached your limit. If the price isn't right, say so and walk out – the vendor will often follow and suggest a compromise price. The more you buy, the better the discount. Once the price is agreed, it is considered bad form to back out of the sale.

In malls and independent shops bargaining is not as expected as in souks and markets. However use your discretion as some shops, such as jewellery stores, smaller electronics stores and eyewear centres do operate a set discount system where the price shown may be 'before discount'. Ask whether there is a discount on the marked price and you may end up with a bargain.

Shipping

With international and local shipping and courier agencies, and both air and sea freight available, shipping anything from a coffee pot to a car is possible. Air freight is faster but more expensive and not really suitable for large or heavy objects, while sea freight may take several weeks to arrive but it is cheaper and, as it's possible to rent containers, size and weight are not so much of an issue. It's worth getting a few quotes from the shipping companies and finding out what will happen when your shipment arrives; some offer no services at the destination while others, usually the bigger ones, will clear customs and deliver to the door. For smaller items, or those that have to be delivered quickly, air freight is better and the items can be tracked. Empost (600 56 5555) offers both local and international courier and air freight services at competitive rates.

Souk Al Arsah

Where To Go For...

An Arabian Shopping Experience

There is nowhere in the UAE better than Sharjah for a chance of getting away from the glitzy malls and international chains, and back to the traditional Arabian souks.

Art

Sharjah is very much at the forefront of the current renaissance in Arabic art and its galleries celebrate both the classical and contemporary. Head to the Sharjah Art Museum for inspiration and advice, then down to Al Qasba for the Maraya Art Centre where both the Barjeel Art Foundation (www.barjeelartfoundation.com) and Shelter (www.shelter.ae) can help with the latest on the local contemporary art scene.

Carpets

Carpets are one of the region's signature items, although they tend to be imported from Afghanistan, Iran, Turkey and Pakistan. The price depends on a number of factors: its origin, the material used, the number of knots, and whether or not it is handmade. The most expensive carpets are usually those handmade with silk in Iran. The higher the quality, the neater the back, so turn the carpets over – if the pattern is clearly depicted and the knots are neat, the carpet is of higher quality than those that are less clear. Try to do some research before you hit the shops so that you have a basic idea of what you are looking for, just in case you come across an unscrupulous dealer. Fortunately, they are the exception and most will happily explain the differences and share their

Traditional Arabian souvenirs

extensive knowledge while seeming to unroll every carpet in the shop for you. Ask to see a selection to get a feel for the differences. Prices range from a few hundred to tens of thousands of dirhams. It is always worth bargaining to get a better price. To find the carpet of your dreams, head to the upper level in the Central Souk (p.150) or to Souk Al Arsah (p.152); there are also carpet shops in the major malls.

Furniture

Sharjah's industrial area is home to two of the UAE's best renowned furniture warehouses. Both Lucky's (06 534 1937) and Pinky's (06 534 1714) sell furniture and accessories sourced mostly from the sub-continent. The dusty warehouses are stacked high with pieces which, once chosen, are oiled and polished before delivery. Prices aren't cheap, but better than similar furniture bought from a shop in a mall, and buying it here is more of an adventure. Cheaper furniture can be found in and around Dhaid where the many carpenters and metalworkers can make almost anything.

Gold

Gold is notably cheaper in the UAE than in Europe, making it a popular souvenir and a main attraction for visitors. It is available in 18, 21, 22 and 24 carats and is sold according to the international gold rate. This means that there should be very little difference in the price if you buy it from a shop in the Central Souk (p.150) or a jewellery shop in the Sahara Centre (p.157). You should do your research before buying anything, especially if you decide to have a piece custom-made to a design, such as a necklace with your name in Arabic.

You'll find a number of jewellery shops in the Central Souk (p.150), mainly in the area closest to Khalid Lagoon, at the Sharjah Gold Centre (p.153) and Souk Al Ghuwair (p.153); branches of local chain, Damas, can be found in most malls, and there are jewellery shops in even the smallest malls.

Souvenirs

From the tacky to the traditional, the range of souvenirs available in Sharjah is staggering. Hand-carved wooden trinket boxes, sometimes filled with oudh (a type of incense) are popular, as are wall hangings from the Central Souk (p.150), khanjars (traditional Arabic daggers), pashminas and keffiyeh headscarves, embroidered slippers, hand-woven carpets and shisha pipes. For the ultimate in Arabian kitsch, pick up a gaudy mosque alarm clock that wakes you up with the sound of the call to prayer – it won't win you any style awards but it's original. The Central Souk (p.150) and Souk Al Arsah (p.152) are great places to look for souvenirs.

Tailoring

If you're in town for longer than a week, it is a great opportunity to get some garments made. Tailors can be found in most areas but the best places to look are along Al Wahda Street for tailors, and around the textile souk and Rolla Square for materials where there is a great selection of textiles available. Alterations and repairs can be made as well as bespoke tailoring.

Souks & Markets

Sharjah's souks have been lovingly preserved and are great places to soak up the atmosphere and pick up a bargain at the same time.

There are a number of souks and markets in Sharjah. The souks are the traditional trading areas, some more formally demarcated than others. In keeping with tradition, bargaining is expected and cash gives the best leverage.

Many of the souks are still found on their original sites by Khalid Lagoon and the creek. Traditionally, souks were where people came to meet, as much as trade. The shaded alleyways were where goods from far and wide were brought to be sold on small stalls, where craftsmen practised their crafts, and where men came to discuss the day's events at the tea and coffee houses.

Sharjah's souks have been preserved and renovated to provide modern conveniences, including air conditioning, to the time honoured consumer experience. In keeping with tradition, Sharjah's souks operate split shift timings, generally opening from 09:30 to 13:30 and from 16:30 to 22:30.

Central Souk

Opened in 1979, the Central Souk is the most famous of Sharjah's traditional markets. The iconic, blue-tiled buildings, topped with windtowers, are widely visible from their position at the creek end of Khalid Lagoon. It is an impressive blend of old and new, with over 600 small shops lining the

Central Souk

two buildings which are connected by store lined footbridges. The shops sell a tantalising array of wares, from the ancient to the modern, from the latest electronics to antiques.

The gold and diamond shops are mostly located in the area closest to the Lagoon. Head up to the first floor for the carpet and curios shops. This is a great place to buy gold, silver and authentic Bedouin jewellery, carpets, crafts and curios, perfumes and pashminas, and so much more.

It is a destination that must be visited during any stay in Sharjah, and once you've bargained over the perfect souvenir, enjoy a break at one of the cafes before heading out for a wander by the Lagoon.

Souk Al Arsah

Souk Al Arsah is probably the oldest market place in the UAE and sits at the edge of the Heritage Area. For many years it was the meeting point for traders from around the Arabian Gulf and from across the Indian Ocean. It was here that the Bedouins would bring their camel trains laden with charcoal and dates to trade for rices, spices and silks from faraway lands.

In the 21st century, visitors can wander the renovated, air-conditioned alleyways, taking in the coral brick walls, the heavy wooden doors, and chatter of the merchants. This is one of the best places in the Emirates to pick up souvenirs and handicrafts, jewellery, textiles, coffee pots, antiques and modern pieces which all make great gifts.

The storekeepers know their wares well and are usually happy to talk about them. A visit to Souk Al Arsah shouldn't be missed and don't forget to take a camera.

Souk Al Bahar

As authentic as it gets, Souk Al Bahar trades today as it has done throughout Sharjah's history and to stroll through the hustle and bustle of this thriving bazaar is to evoke the past. The souk runs parallel to the creek and one can imagine how busy it would have been when dhows lined the creek here, being laden with goods destined for India, Pakistan and Iran.

The small shops sell a staggering variety of products including herbs and spices, textiles and clothes (including traditional Emirati abayas), furniture, perfumes and frankincense, sacks of rice, shisha pipes and their flavoured tobaccos. Don't forget your camera!

Souk Al Ghuwair

Also known as Rolla Market, this area is divided into markets which are always open late. There is an eclectic combination of products on sale, from gold and textiles to hardware and electrical items, and even luggage. This is a busy area of the city and parking can be a challenge.

Sharjah Gold Centre

Located on Al Wahda Road, the Gold Centre is a great destination if you're looking to add a little sparkle to your life. Housing branches of some of the country's top jewellery shops as well as independent stores, the high quality and great variety can be very hard to resist. Items can be made to any design and the jewellers will be happy to offer advice. Great deals can be picked up here but you will have to bargain hard.

Fish Souk

Fish don't get much fresher than those on display at the Fish Souk. Located next to the Khalid Lagoon, where the fishing boats come in, it's a great place to absorb some local colour and to get an idea of the sheer variety of fish caught in Gulf waters, great for photo opportunities too. If you're looking to buy your dinner, the fish can be cleaned and gutted on site, and don't forget to bargain.

Fruit & Vegetable Souk

The Fruit & Vegetable Souk is on the other side of the road from the Fish Souk and bustles throughout the day. There's a great selection of produce on display and, as in all souks, the prices are not fixed – the greater the quantity, the greater the discount.

Pot & Plant Souk

Rising above it all, the Pot & Plant Souk looks down on the frantic pace of the Fish Souk and Fruit & Vegetable Souk, from the road bridge to the creek. The pace of life is gentler up here and the vendors are happy to give advice. The shops sell everything you'll need, whether you are looking for trees or indoor plants – the smaller pots make great souvenirs too.

East Coast Fish Souks

The fish markets of Kalba, Khor Fakkan and Dibba Al Hisn are fantastic finds. Immaculately clean with the freshest of fish and an array of fruit, vegetables and meat these are great places to visit with a camera or shopping basket.

AL BAHRAIN CARPETS & ANTIQUE NOV.
050 6465126
البحرين لتجارة السجاد والتحف

Shopping Malls

Great for so much more than just shopping, Sharjah's malls are places for eating, meeting and entertainment with attractions for all ages.

Mega Mall

06 574 2574
Al Estiqlal St   www.sharjahmegamall.com

Located in the streets of Abu Shagara, Mega Mall has over 150 shops spread over three floors. Big international names Bhs, Zara, Mango and Promod sit alongside Jack Jones, Guess and regional favourite, Paris Gallery.

For the weary shopper there is a large food court and plenty of cafes to choose from – Mugg and Bean makes for a refreshing alternative to the usual suspects. If the younger family members have shopped till they dropped, a quick trip to Antic's Land will soon revive them. The rides and edutainment activities will keep them amused, and look out for the snakes; take a walk through the boat and remember to look up!

The supermarket, on the ground floor, is open 24 hours and there is plenty of underground parking.

Map 1 E3

Safeer Mall

06 531 3366
Al Ittihad St   www.safeermall.com

Safeer Mall is on Al Ittihad Street, the main road from Sharjah to Dubai, close to the Al Nahda residential district. The three-storey mall is anchored by a huge Sharaf DG electronics store and Home Mart furniture and interiors shop; and there are branches of Max and Splash for clothes. The gym chain, Fitness First, have both men's and ladies facilities on the second floor, just below Space City, a family entertainment venue with a large soft play area.

A hypermarket is also attached to the mall. There is plenty of underground parking and a pay to park scheme. **Map** 1 C3

Sahara Centre

06 531 6611
Al Nahda St   www.sahara-centre.com

Sahara Centre opened in 2002, and is located in the Al Nahda residential area, just off the Sharjah to Dubai highway; it remains one Sharjah's most popular destinations. The distinctive 'tented' architecture makes it hard to miss and it is a major landmark.

The mall offers a great range of international stores and regional chains as well as entertainment venues for all the family. Over 190 stores can be found within the bright and airy interior, big international names like Debenhams, Marks & Spencer and Toys R Us, sit alongside premier local brands, Spinneys supermarket, THE One and Marina Furniture.

Adventureland is an indoor family entertainment area which offers a fantastic selection of games and rides, including a roller coaster and water flume. If you enjoy a more passive experience, visitors can take in a movie at Grand Cinemas, and with a multicultural food court there's sure to be something to suit all tastes and ages. There is plenty of parking and the mall is well served by buses and taxis throughout the day. **Map** 1 B4

Sharjah City Centre

06 532 7700

Al Wahda St · www.sharjahcitycentre.com

Sharjah City Centre has been extended and revamped in recent years and is now home to well over 100 shops. Centrally located, on Al Wahda Street, the mall boasts international anchor stores, H&M, Monsoon and New Look for clothes, Carrefour hypermarket and Borders bookshop. For younger shoppers, there's Mothercare and a huge Babyshop; they're also well catered for with the arcades and attractions of Magic Planet when they're shopped out.

The food court on the first floor is impressive and there are cafes throughout. Car rental and courier services counters can be found and there are customer service desks at the centre of the ground floor.

As well as good parking and bus connections a dedicated taxi drop-off and pick-up point is to be found near the New Look entrance. **Map** 1 D4

Other Malls

There are several smaller malls throughout Sharjah emirate which typically include grocery, pharmacy, jewellery, electrical and toy stores, as well as a cafeteria or food court. These are often convenient spots to head to for essentials and may also house an ATM machine.

The Sharjah Cooperatives are great destinations for all shopping essentials with a full supermarket range as well as offering pharmacy, financial and travel services.

There are smaller shopping centres in the east coast and hinterland towns which fully cater for their communities.

Sharjah has spacious modern shopping malls

Independent Stores

Malls are a relatively new concept in Sharjah and before them, international, regional and local brands set up shop along the city's main roads. Cafes, bakeries, small grocery shops and mobile phone shops can be found on pretty much every street. On Al Qassima Street are branches of Babyshop (06 533 2242) and Home Center (06 566 8899).

If you're in the market for a tent, or possibly a marquee, then Al Wahda Road, near Safeer Mall, is the area to head for; try Al Baddad Tents (06 531 3050). Alternatively head out of town and try one of the many specialists that line the roads surrounding Al Dhaid and Al Madam.

Other favourite items for independent shops within the emirate are pots, plants, carpets, tents, inflatables, buckets and ceramic pots. Many make good gifts, or at least talking points, and buying in these shops provides great opportunities to hone your bargaining skills.

Some of the best marketplaces are found on the east coast and in the hinterland towns. Amongst these independent shopping areas are some great food shops, specialising in local honey, Omani sweets or other local produce. The fish, fruit and vegetable markets are also fantastic places to visit and to shop at.

If you're shopping for children, Book Mall (06 574 9555) at Al Qasba has a great selection of Usborne books (and a very comfy area to browse them in) and the shop at Sharjah Aquarium (06 528 5288) is stocked with an interesting and unusual selection of goodies to please young and old. There are also good shops at most of the other main attractions.

The many sides of shopping in Sharjah

Going Out

Dining Out

Enjoy a culinary journey through Sharjah; from street food to fine dining, there's something for every taste and budget.

Dining out in the Middle East is traditionally a very social affair, whether at home with extended family and friends or out in a large group. People tend to go out fairly late too, so you may have the restaurant to yourself if you like to eat before nine or ten.

It is possible to eat your way around the world in Sharjah, from the fine dining international restaurants of the top hotels to the well-known fast food chains, pavement shawarma stands and classic Indian and Pakistani curry houses. Whatever your budget you're in for a treat.

Hospitality is a national trait and there is a special enthusiasm and generosity to traditional Arabic cuisine that sets it apart from others around the world; this is after all, the culture that brought the world coffee and doughnuts, or khawa (coffee) and awamat (fried balls of dough rolled in syrup).

For a taste of Arabia, head for one of Sharjah's great Arabic restaurants; specifically Emirati cuisine is a little harder to find but is showcased at special events, including the Al Qasba Food Festival and National Day celebrations.

Alcohol and pork are not available in the emirate of Sharjah.

Arabian Experience

The Arabic custom is for everybody to share a veritable feast of dishes, served in communal bowls. The meal is traditionally presented on platters, placed on mats on the floor in the centre of the circle of guests; large Arabic flat breads are often used in place of plates. Diners then take food from the communal plates with their hands, using only their right hand.

Sharjah's culinary heritage reflects the emirate's position as a regional trading hub. Traditional Emirati cuisine relied on a few simple ingredients but drew on influences from Iran to India, Afghanistan to Africa, with great emphasis placed on a variety of herbs and spices, fruits and nuts. Dried limes are a common ingredient, reflecting a Persian influence; they impart a distinctively musty, tangy, sour flavour to soups and stews. Spices such as cinnamon, saffron and turmeric along with nuts (almonds or pistachios) and dried fruit add interesting flavours to Emirati dishes.

Delicious varieties of breads, dips and mezzeh come from the simplest ingredients, from the ubiquitous hummus to the fava bean stew, ful medammes but many of the dishes are of disputed origin. However, the cosmopolitan influences have made Sharjah food something special. Specialities include Al Harees, a celebratory dish made from meat and wheat, slow-cooked in a clay pot or oven for hours, the spiced rice and meat dish, machbous, and the slow-roasted, stuffed lamb dish, khouzi; a wide variety of seafood graces traditional menus, too. The evocative, tangy spice mixtures unique to Sharjah reflects its history, and its baharat and za'atar mixes vary from elsewhere in the region.

Street Food

The shawarma is to Sharjah what the hot dog is to New York. The popular snack, consisting of rolled pita bread filled with lamb or chicken carved from a rotating spit, can be found throughout the city, and tiny cafeterias serving the delicacy are on most streets. At around Dhs.5 each, they're the perfect fast food. Many cafeterias will also sell falafel, a great option for vegetarians. Street-side cafeterias also squeeze some of the best and least expensive fresh juices in the city.

Vegetarian

There are plenty of delicious local delicacies that will thrill herbivores. Rahib salad, a hot combination of aubergine and tomato, makes a great side dish when eating Lebanese food, as do tabouleh, fattoush and falafel, all served with fluffy fresh bread.

What's more, the huge population of South Asians means there are plenty of authentic vegetable curries to be found in Sharjah; try a vegetable thali, which consists of up to 10 small pots of curries, pickles and sauces into which you can mix rice or dip into with chapatti. Sharjah's souks are great places to wander in and to absorb the atmosphere and aroma of the spices and other ingredients central to the cuisine. Once your senses and appetite have been whetted, enjoy the authentic flavours of Sharjah at any of the many events and festivals that take place throughout the year. All festivities are accompanied by food stalls showcasing traditional dishes. Hotels and tour operators can also often arrange desert trips to try traditional food in a traditional setting.

Sharjah Golf & Shooting Club

Entertainment

With cinemas, theatres, festivals and the dedicated Arts and Heritage area, there's always something exciting going on in Sharjah for all ages.

Cinema

A trip to the movies is a perennially popular pastime in the Emirates; and it's a great way to escape the heat in the summer. Cinemas are open seven days a week, with evening weekend showings particularly popular; there are often extra shows late at night on weekends, too. Cinema listings and timings can be found in daily newspapers and on individual cinema websites.

Sharjah's multi-screen cinemas are mostly found in the main shopping malls; be sure to take warm clothes as the air conditioning in cinemas is notoriously arctic. Tickets cost between Dhs.30 and Dhs.40.

In general, the cinemas show mainstream Hollywood, Bollywood and Arabic films. Special showings are sometimes on the programme at Al Qasba

Family Friendly

A fascinating and friendly place for all the family, there are attractions and activities to suit all ages.

There is a regular programme of children focused events and shows, particularly at Al Qasba, and all venues and festivals have dedicated play areas for the little ones.

though; for example, The Magic Lantern is a film club for six to 12 year olds, which aims to introduce them to popular new films and classics from around the world (screenings are held on Saturdays).

Festivals

There are fantastic events going on all year round in Sharjah. Many visitors travel specifically to attend these events but they also make great days out for anyone already in town. The biggest are the Sharjah Light Festival (an unmatched light and music illumination of the city's landscape and buildings), Sharjah Theatre Days (for traditional and contemporary storytelling), Sharjah Heritage Days (for an exciting insight into the past), Family Fun (for entertaining all ages), Al Qasba Food Festival (for international gourmet treats), and the end of year spectacular that is the Sharjah Water Festival (carnival, circus, musical extravaganza and world-class sporting event in one). All the festivals feature attractions for all ages, including food stalls, musical performances, children's play areas, heritage displays, parades and, of course, a friendly and welcoming atmosphere. See p.48 for details.

Theatre

Theatre and the performing arts are highly regarded in Sharjah. The Sharjah National Theatre was established in 1978 and every March the longstanding Sharjah Theatre Days festival celebrates this theatrical tradition. Shows promote traditional storytelling practices, retell classical stories and showcase new work with performances aimed at all ages.

Al Qasba

There is so much to do along Al Qasba's kilometre of canal, walkway, and shopping and dining arcade that families often spend an entire day here.

Located in the heart of Sharjah, along a canal built to join the bases of Al Khan Lagoon and Khalid Lagoon, Al Qasba is a unique arts, culture and family destination. The entertainment hub is watched over by the Eye of the Emirates, a 60m high Ferris wheel that affords excellent views across the Sharjah rooftops and over the lagoon to Dubai; no trip to Al Qasba would be complete without a ride in one of the 42 air-conditioned cabins. Below the Ferris wheel are the dancing fountains. A firm favourite with children of all ages, they are free to play among the shoots and sprays of water between the performances when the fountains 'dance' in time to music; don't forget a towel.

Open all day every day, the waterside walkways and alfresco eateries really come to life in the evenings. By day it is peaceful, the place hums gently with business lunches, laptop coffee breaks and mothers' groups. By night, the lively buzz sees families promenading and making the most of the chance to dine al fresco. There are cafes and restaurants from around the world. Familiar coffee shop chains rub shoulders with sushi from Japan, Arabic food from Syria and Lebanon, seafood from Greece, curries from India and Thailand, pizza and pasta from Italy, and peri-peri chicken from Portugal. No

Al Qasba at night

visit is complete without trying the extraordinary juices and ice cream flavours on offer at the many speciality outlets.

There are four-wheel cycles for hire and traditional boats, abras, take trips along the canal and round the lagoons. As well as the restaurants and cafes there is a garden centre, bookshop, photography studio and an impressive gallery and art hub. Al Qasba is renowned as a festival, performance and exhibition venue for contemporary visual arts. The Maraya Art Centre has three levels of gallery space dedicated to multimedia, Arab art and Contemporary Art. From food festivals to classic car exhibitions and children's cinema, there's always something happening at Al Qasba, for more information see www.qaq.ae.

Restaurants

Take a trip around the culinary world in the gastronomic melting pot that is Sharjah and don't miss the emirate's top alfresco dining destination.

Whatever your taste and no matter how limited or unlimited your budget, you're sure to find something to suit in Sharjah's restaurant scene. From the small, street-side shawarma stands to the top hotels, the eateries of Sharjah are popular throughout the day but really come to life at night.

As a melting pot of cultures and cuisines, Sharjah plays host to a plethora of great restaurants, from Arabic to Indian, Italian and Thai. The seafood restaurants shouldn't be missed; they make the most of the city's coastal position to ensure the freshest catch is served. From great meaty hammour, to succulent prawns, rich-tasting crab, sparklingly fresh kingfish and delicate shaari, the fresh produce available to Sharjah's seafood restaurants is superb. The alfresco dining hotspot, Al Qasba (p.170) is the perfect destination if you're having trouble deciding which cuisine to go for as the range on offer will please everyone – even the children, who are well catered for with entertainment as well dining options.

Over on the east coast there are several fantastic little eateries, particularly at the impressive fish markets. Beit Al Nokhetha in Kalba is a superb restaurant right on the beach. There are also well respected options at the Oceanic Hotel and Breeze Motel, see Exploring The East Coast, p.98.

Al Arsah Coffee Shop
Souk Al Arsah

Arabic/Middle Eastern
06 568 0903

Take a break from shopping to sample the biryani and juice at the cafe at heart of the traditional Al Arsah Souk. This is one of the oldest souks in the UAE so there can be few more authentic places to stop for a bite. **Map** 6 C9

Al Dente
Coral Beach Resort

Italian
06 522 9999

Al Dente is the resort's signature restaurant. The focus is on great Italian dishes, using the best seasonal ingredients. The portions are generous so make sure you go hungry and don't forget to leave room for dessert. **Map** 1 K1

Bangkok Town
Nr Grand Cinema, Buheira Corniche

Southeast Asian
06 556 8282

Hidden on a quiet corner just off the corniche, this unassuming Thai restaurant is famed amongst Sharjah's foodies for its exceptional cuisine and friendly service. The Yam Pla Dook Foo (a crispy fish salad) has been known to draw devotees across from other emirates just for the one dish. **Map** 1 D2

Calypso
Radisson Blu Hotel

International
06 565 7777

A great spot for an alfresco lunch or early dinner, this outdoor restaurant overlooks the resort's swimming pools, beach and out to sea. The simple menu concentrates on classic snacks and there is a great selection of freshly squeezed juices and smoothies. **Map** 1 G1

Canton
Chinese

Radisson Blu Hotel
06 565 7777

Authentic Chinese favourites are created by the top master chefs at the Radisson Blu's oriental haven. Try the chefs' specialities if you're feeling a little more adventurous. The food presentation and the general service are impressive. **Map** 1 G1

Casa Samak
Seafood

Coral Beach Resort
06 522 9999

Perhaps the best location of all the seafood restaurants, it is set fair in the shade of tall palm trees on the edge of a sandy beach, with views straight out to sea. The menu is suitably straightforward, featuring the freshest produce simply and perfectly cooked. **Map** 1 K1

Fish Corner
Seafood

Al Qasba
06 556 8884

Fish Corner features a fishmonger style counter where diners can select the freshest fish before deciding whether to have it baked, steamed, grilled, sauteed or deep-fried; and then choosing from an array of sauces. **Map** 7 G8

Flavours of Asia
Southeast Asian

Sharjah Golf & Shooting Club
06 548 7777

Surrounded by the lush green of the golf course, Flavours of Asia draws its influences from China, India, Japan and Mongolia to present a wide selection of dishes, healthy juices, speciality teas and appetising desserts. **Map** 1 K7

Flavours of Sharjah

Gazebo

Indian

King Faisal Road

06 553 2999

Gazebo is renowned for its vegetarian and non-vegetarian dishes. The friendly, knowledgeable waiters are happy to make recommendations and help you through the menu of creamy and delicately spiced curries, or meat from the tandoor, all accompanied by a refreshing glass of Lassi (made from chilled yoghurt). Map 1 E3

Kamat Vegetarian Restaurant

Indian

King Faisal Road

06 559 9044

Vegetarian dishes from north and south India are served by friendly staff in this low cost Sharjah favourite. The vegetable kebabs, dosas, samosas, paneer malai tikka and thali all come recommended. Chinese food is also available. Map 1 E3

Lemongrass

Southeast Asian

Al Qasba

06 556 5366

Located in the dining hub that is Al Qasba, Lemongrass offers an extensive menu of tantalising Thai treats. Good for vegetarians as well as meat and seafood lovers, the setting is friendly, the prices are reasonable and the portions are generous. Map 7 G8

Masala Craft

Indian

Al Qasba

06 556 6284

The antique swinging chairs outside this restaurant are a good indication of the quality and authenticity of the cooking inside. The menu celebrates many well-known classic dishes but also offers a selection of house specialities which, although lesser known, are packed full of flavour. It is well worth experimenting here and asking for the waiter's advice on the day. **Map** 7 H10

Sammach
Sharjah Aquarium

Seafood
06 528 0095

Where better for a seafood restaurant than an aquarium? It's open from noon till late, making it a great place for dinner, as well as a post Aquarium trip bite. As would be expected, seafood features heavily on the menu but there are alternatives. This is a peaceful corner of Sharjah which shouldn't be missed. **Map** 1 C1

Al Sanobar
Al Khan Road

Seafood
06 528 3501

This atmospheric Lebanese restaurant specialises in local seafood served alongside traditional specialities of flatbread, hummus and pickles. The ceiling and walls are decorated with nets and other fishing paraphernalia. **Map** 1 C1

Sensi
Sharjah Golf & Shooting Club

Italian
06 548 7777

Sensi serves a taste of Italy from the clubhouse looking out over the greens and fairways of the golf course. Some of the menu changes on a regular basis, but seafood is a speciality and make sure to leave room for pudding. They also serve a colourful selection of fruit cocktails, many of which could be a meal on their own. **Map** 1 K7

Shababeek

Arabic/Middle Eastern

Al Qasba   06 554 0444

Once drawn in by the patterned purple interior, marvel as the chefs prepare an amazing Lebanese menu. The food is exceptional and includes some fantastic lamb specialities. A wonderful combination is the lamb saj with their special house lemonade which, made with rosewater and grenadine, tastes just like Turkish Delight. **Map** 7 G9

Shiraz

Iranian

Corniche Al Buhaira Hotel   06 519 2222

A hidden treasure; sample authentic Iranian food prepared in an open kitchen, while taking in the great views across the city. This restaurant specialises in the classics of Persian cuisine with incredible and authentic kebabs and rice dishes. **Map** 1 D2

Stefano's

Italian

Al Qasba   06 556 0969

Great for the whole family, dine alfresco and enjoy their ever popular pasta and pizzas; then indulge in a spot of people watching over the amazing Tiramisu dessert. The regular lunch time offers and buffets offer great value. **Map** 7 G9

Sumo Sushi & Bento

Southeast Asian

Al Qasba   06 556 9493

Serving up intricate sushi dishes, salads and the famous Japanese Bento (lunchbox) menus from a prime spot overlooking the canal and attractions of Al Qasba, this is a great choice for an evening out. **Map** 7 G9

Shiraz, Corniche Al Buhaira Hotel

Cafes

Kahwa or cappuccino; arty, alfresco or internet; Sharjah has embraced cafe culture with gusto and there is a busy, buzzing scene.

Arabia introduced the world to coffee, so it is fitting that a good mix of big international chains and small independent coffee shops are to be found throughout Sharjah, in the malls, hotels and at Al Qasba. Don't miss the opportunity to try some of the smaller cafes and coffee shops for an authentic taste of Arabia. Visitors are often offered sweetened mint tea by the vendors in carpet shops and it is considered good form to accept.

Al Nofara

Al Qasba   06 554 2667

Inside this Syrian cafe is a fountain surrounded with tables and armchairs, perfect for escaping the heat of the day and enjoying their amazing sweets and coffees. During the cooler months there is plenty of pleasant outdoor seating. Map 7 G10

Art Museum Cafe

Sharjah Art Museum   06 568 8222

With funky booth seating and a good selection of cakes and sandwiches, this is a great secret hangout. The museum's library opens on to the cafe and has a collection of over 4,000 titles to choose to peruse with your coffee. Map 6 D9

Traditional tastes for tea, coffee and nuts have created a vibrant cafe culture

Cafes

Bert's Parisian Cafe

Al Qasba   06 556 6861

Overlooking the children's play area, this is a very popular spot for parents to enjoy a coffee and croissant while watching their kids play. Inside it is a cool, dark atmosphere with piles of magazines and newspapers, comfortable sofas and armchairs and quiet corners to while away the days in. **Map** 7 H8

Cafe at the Falls

Radisson Blu Hotel   06 5565 7777

Set in the extraordinary atrium of Sharjah's top hotel this is a rainforest cafe complete with waterfall. The indoor forest makes for a remarkable setting and the cafe is a popular spot throughout the day with specials at breakfast and lunch and a great selection of snacks. **Map** 1 G1

Gerard's Café

Al Qasba   06 556 0428

This local French patisserie serves traditional delicacies including cakes, pastries and croissants, all freshly baked and popular throughout the day. **Map** 7 G8

Sharjah Museum of Islamic Civilization Cafe

Corniche Street   06 565 5455

On the top floor is a luxurious cafe dramatically set underneath the building's majestic dome which is dark blue on the inside, ornately detailing the night sky. It is the perfect place to recline in an armchair and contemplate the museum's story of faith, science and art. **Map** 1 F1

Cafe at the Falls, Radisson Blu Hotel

Index

Mini Visitors' Guides

Perfect pocket-sized visitors' guides

Activity Guides

Drive, trek, dive and swim... life will never
be boring again

Explorer Products

Check out www.explorerpublishing.com

Mini Maps
Fit the city in your pocket

Maps
Never get lost again

Photography Books
Beautiful cities caught through the lens

Practical & Lifestyle Products & Calendars
The perfect accessories for a buzzing lifestyle

EXPLORER

Publishing
Founder & CEO Alistair MacKenzie
Associate Publisher Claire England

Editorial
Editors Matt Warnock,
Siobhan Campbell, Jo Iivonen
Corporate Editor Charlie Scott
Web Editor Laura Coughlin
Production Coordinator
Kathryn Calderon
Production Assistant
Janette Tamayo
Senior Editorial Assistant
Mimi Stankova
Editorial Assistant Ingrid Cupido,
Amapola Castillo

Design & Photography
Creative Director Pete Maloney
Art Director Ieyad Charaf
Contract Publishing Manager
Chris Goldstraw
Designer Michael Estrada
Junior Designer Didith Hapiz
Layout Manager Jayde Fernandes
Layout Designers Mansoor Ahmed,
Shawn Zuzarte
Cartography Manager
Zainudheen Madathil
Maps Administrator Ikumi Merola
Cartographers Noushad Madathil,
Sunita Lakhiani
Image Editor Henry Hilos

Sales & Marketing
Group Media Sales Manager
Peter Saxby

Media Sales Area Managers
Laura Zuffa, Pouneh Hafizi
Corporate Sales Area Manager
Hannah Brisby
Media Sales Executive Bryan Anes
Marketing Manager Lindsay Main
Sales & Marketing Assistant
Shedan Ebona
Group Retail Sales Manager
Ivan Rodrigues
Senior Retail Sales Merchandisers
Ahmed Mainodin, Firos Khan
Retail Sales Merchandisers
Johny Mathew, Shan Kumar
Retail Sales Coordinator
Michelle Mascarenhas
Retail Sales Drivers Shabsir Madathil,
Najumudeen K.I.
Warehouse Assistant Mohamed Haji

Finance & Administration
Administration Manager
Fiona Hepher
Accountant Cherry Enriquez
Accounts Assistants Sunil Suvarna
Melody Beato
Reception & Admin Assistant
Marie Joy Abarquez
Personnel Relations Officer
Rafi Jamal
Office Assistant Shafeer Ahamed

IT & Digital Solutions
Digital Solutions Manager
Derrick Pereira
Senior IT Administrator R. Ajay
Web Developer Anas Abdul Latheef

Contact Us

▶ Register Online
Check out our new website for event listings, competitions and
Abu Dhabi and Dubai info, and submit your own restaurant reviews.
Log onto **www.explorerpublishing.com**

▶ Newsletter
Register online to receive Explorer's monthly newsletter and be
first in line for our special offers and competitions.
Log onto **www.explorerpublishing.com**

▶ General Enquiries
We'd love to hear your thoughts and answer any questions
you have about this book or any other Explorer product.
Contact us at **info@explorerpublishing.com**

▶ Careers
If you fancy yourself as an Explorer, send your CV (stating the
position you're interested in) to **jobs@explorerpublishing.com**

▶ Contract Publishing
For enquiries about Explorer's Contract Publishing arm and design
services contact **contracts@explorerpublishing.com**

▶ PR & Marketing
For enquiries contact **marketing@explorerpublishing.com**

▶ Maps
For cartography enquiries, including orders and comments, contact
maps@explorerpublishing.com

▶ Media and Corporate Sales
For bulk sales and customisation options, for this book or any
Explorer product, contact **sales@explorerpublishing.com**

Notes